AF477779

SCOTT LYALL

THE POWER BALL

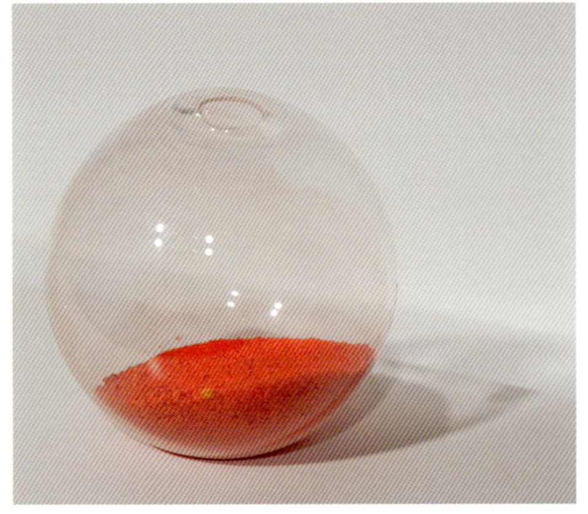

SCOTT LYALL

THE 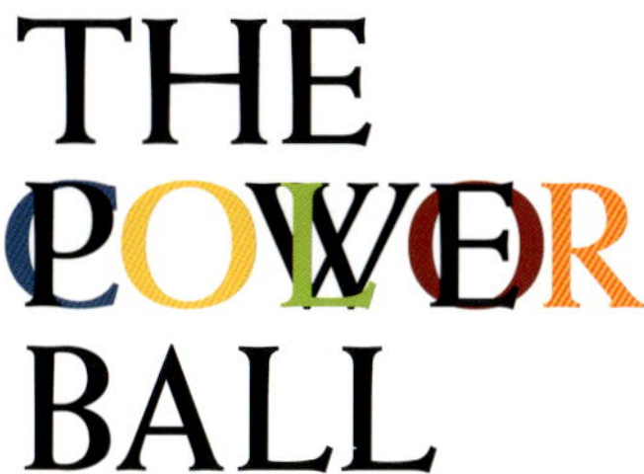POWER BALL

Curated by Gregory Burke

COMMISSIONING
PARTNER

The
Power
Plant

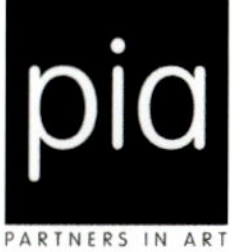pia
PARTNERS IN ART

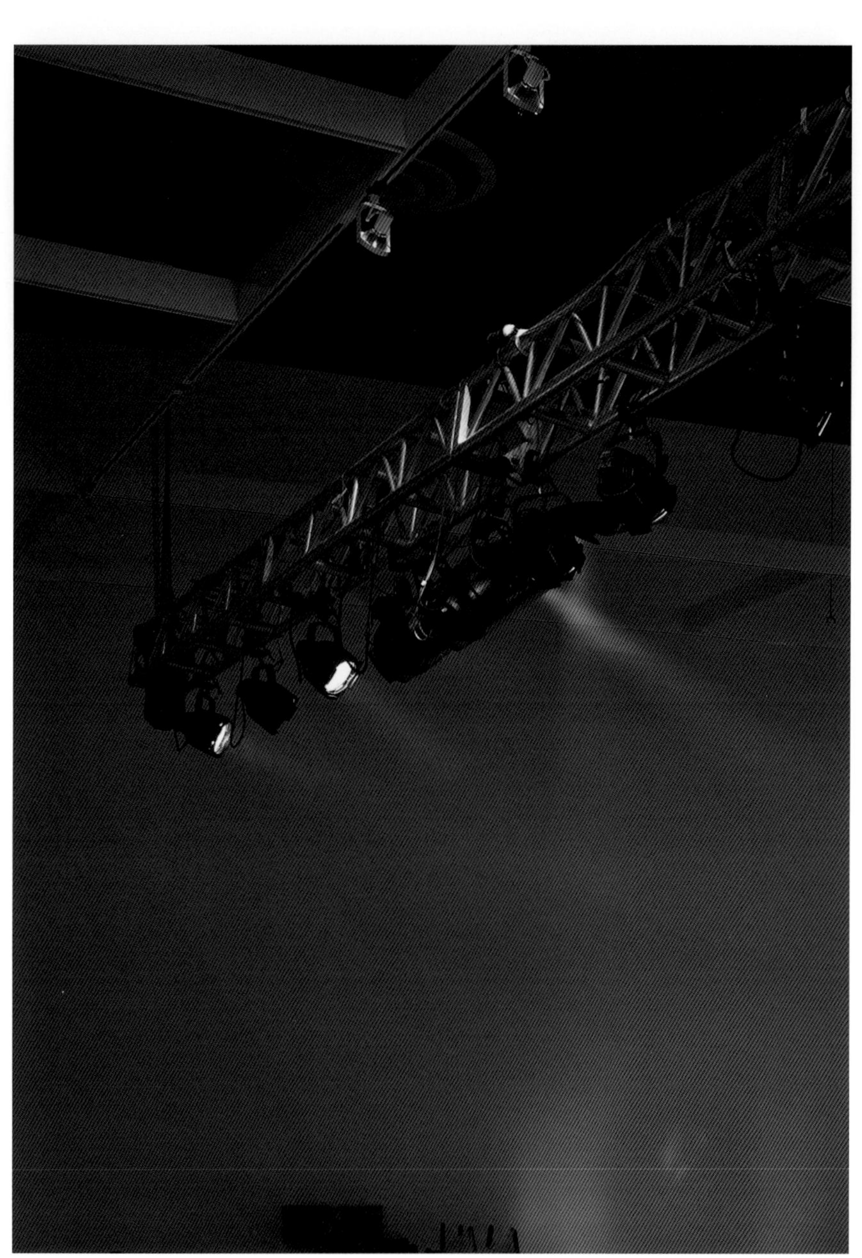

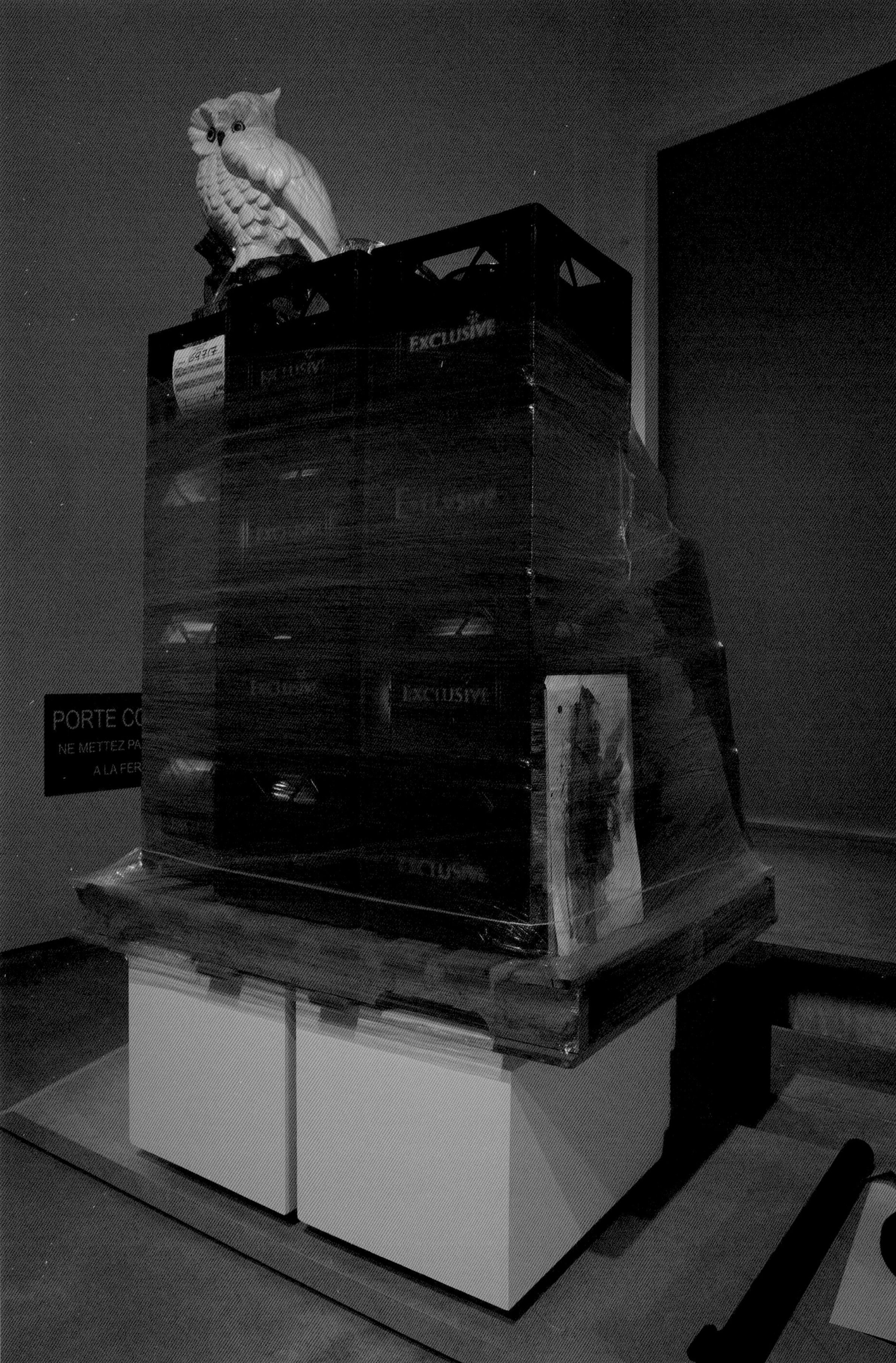
EXCLUSIVE
PORTE CO
NE METTEZ PA
A LA FER

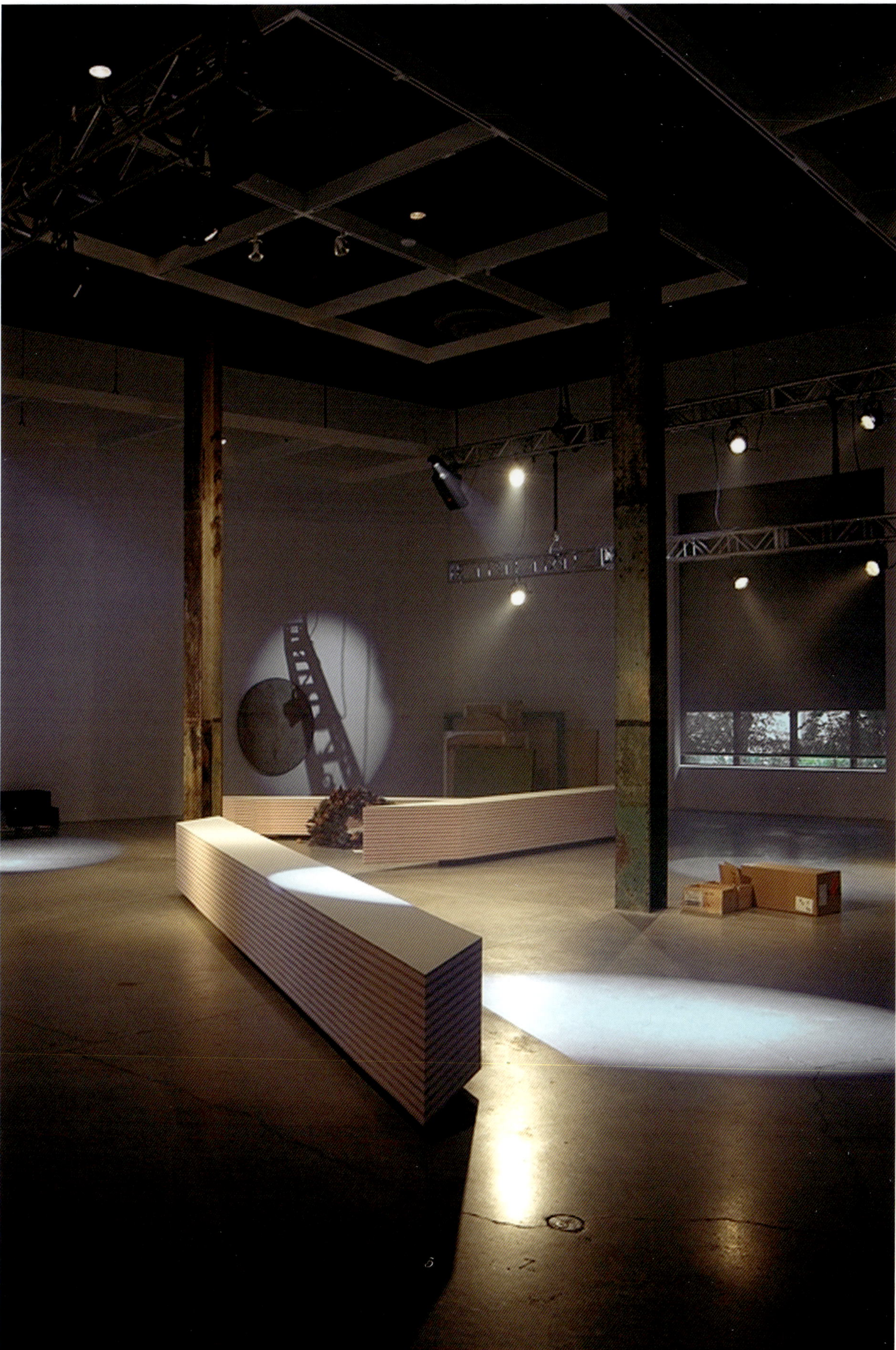

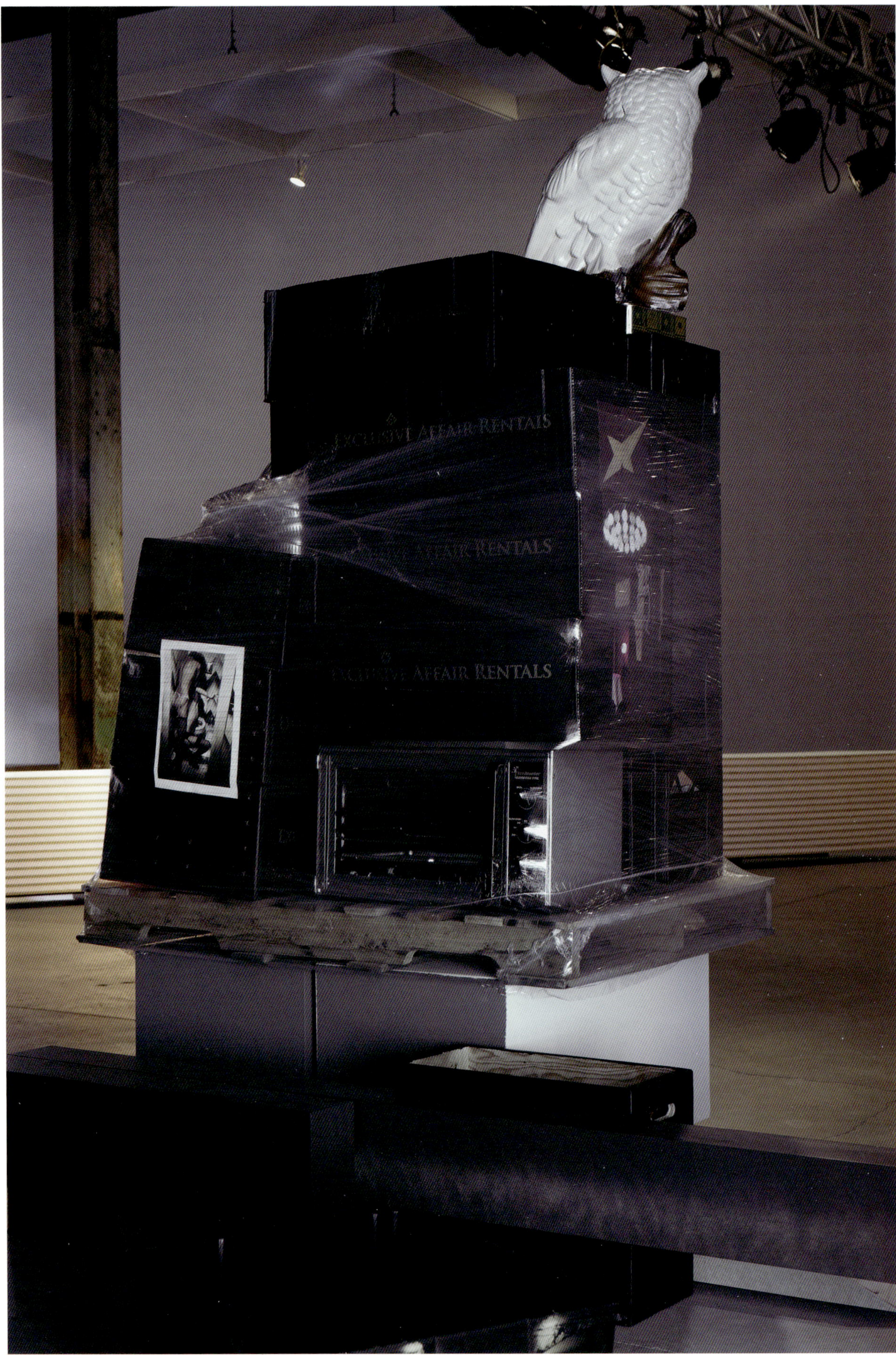
EXCLUSIVE AFFAIR RENTALS
EXCLUSIVE AFFAIR RENTALS
EXCLUSIVE AFFAIR RENTALS

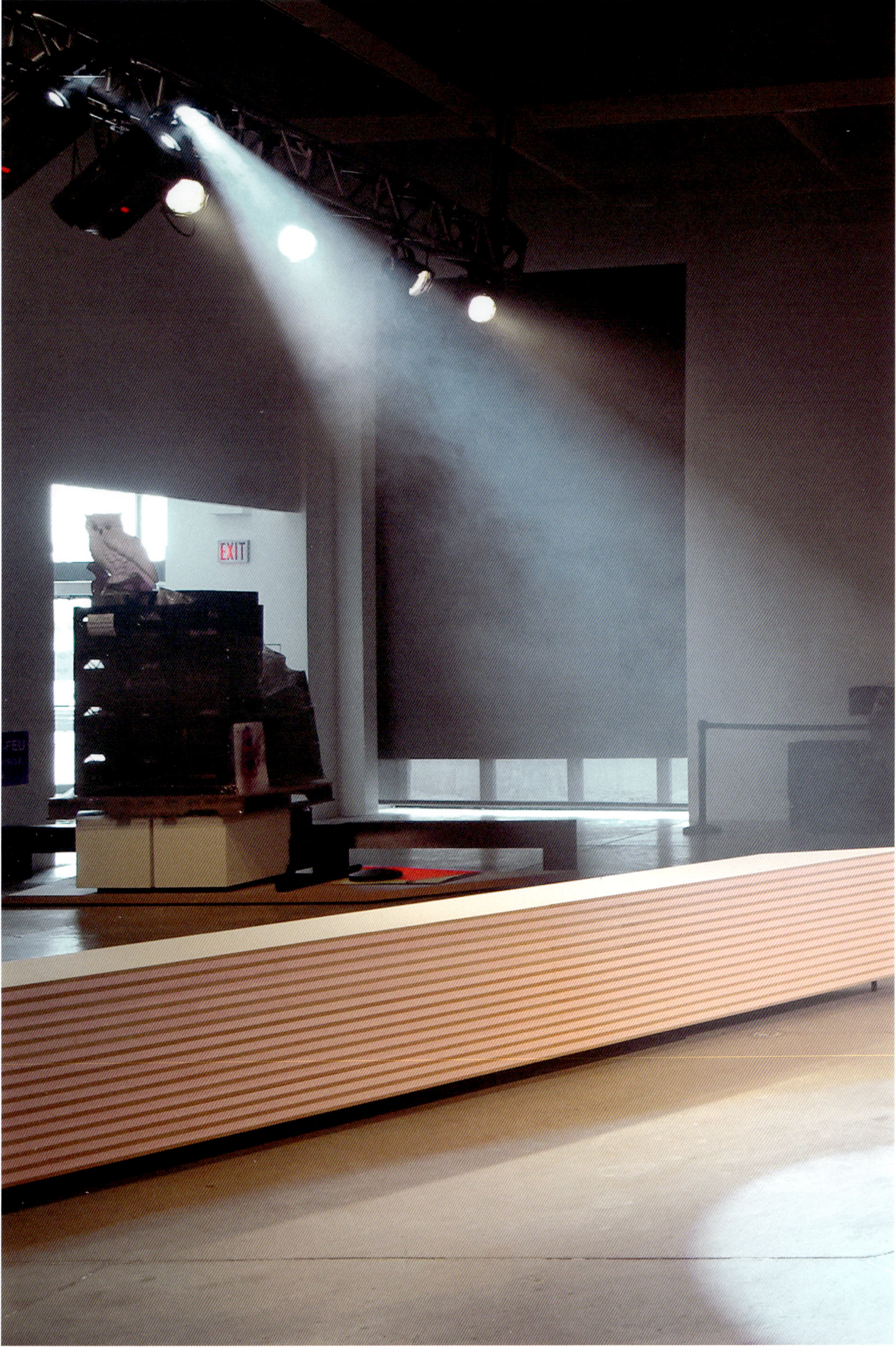
EXIT

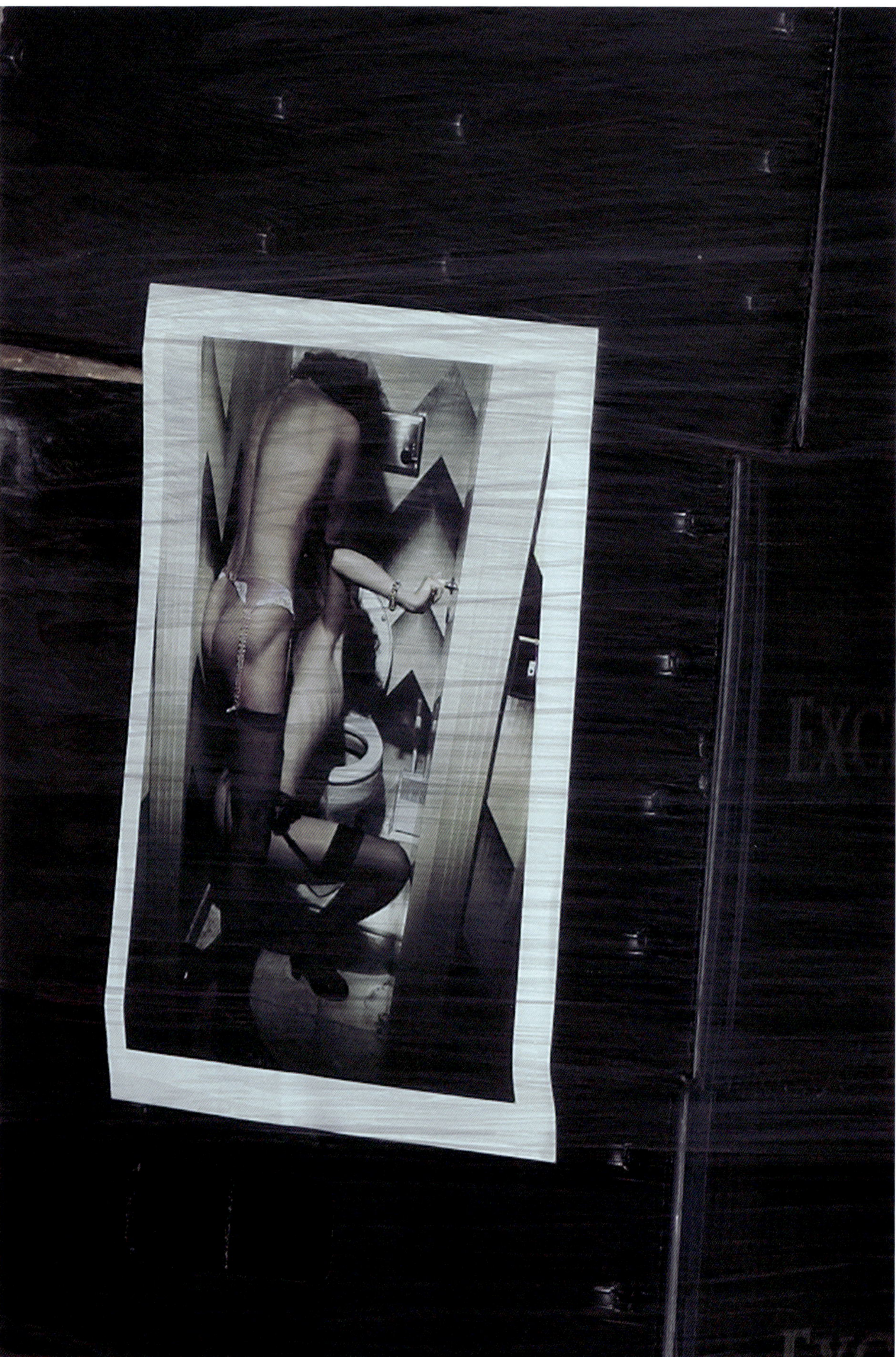

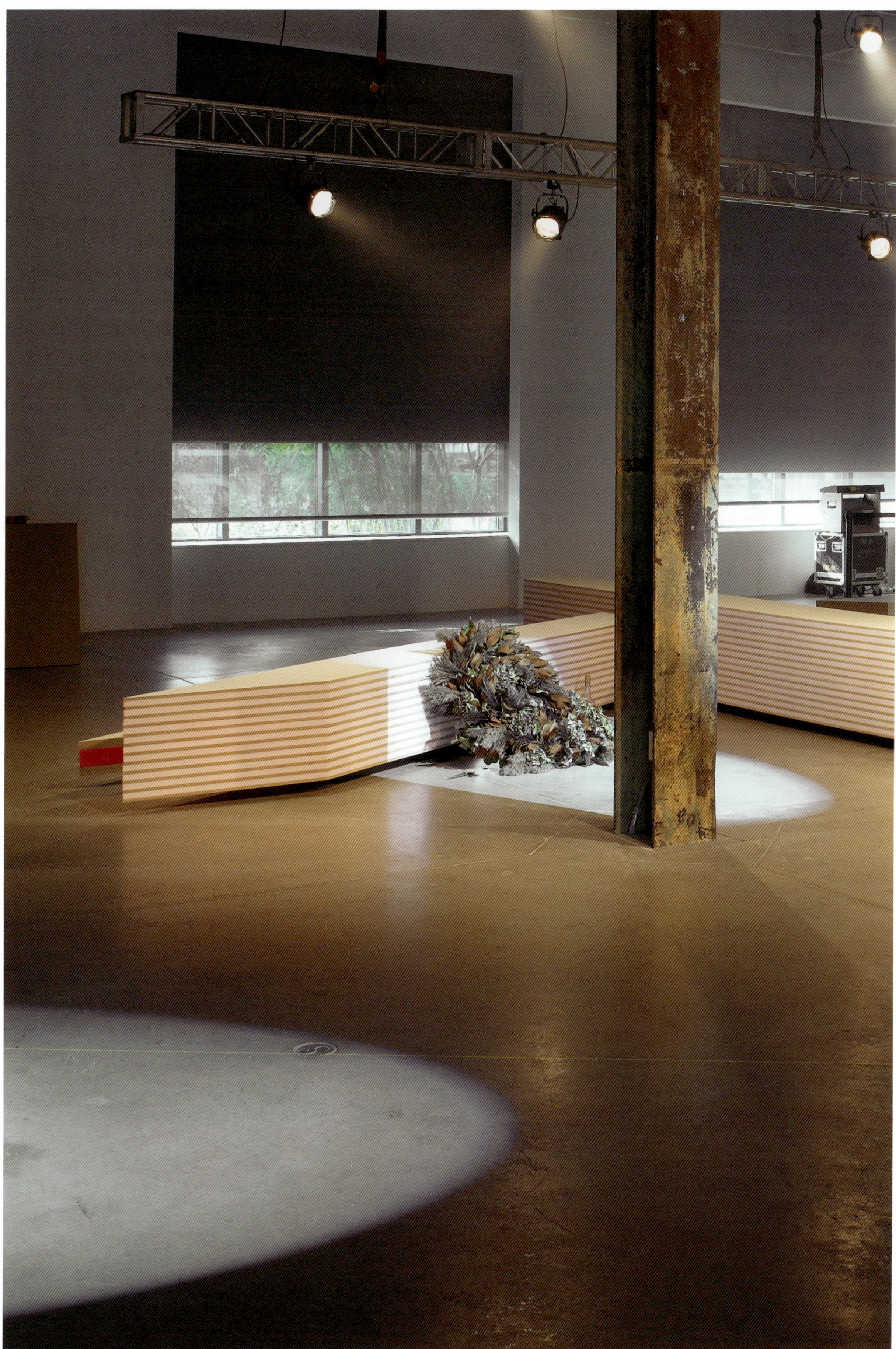

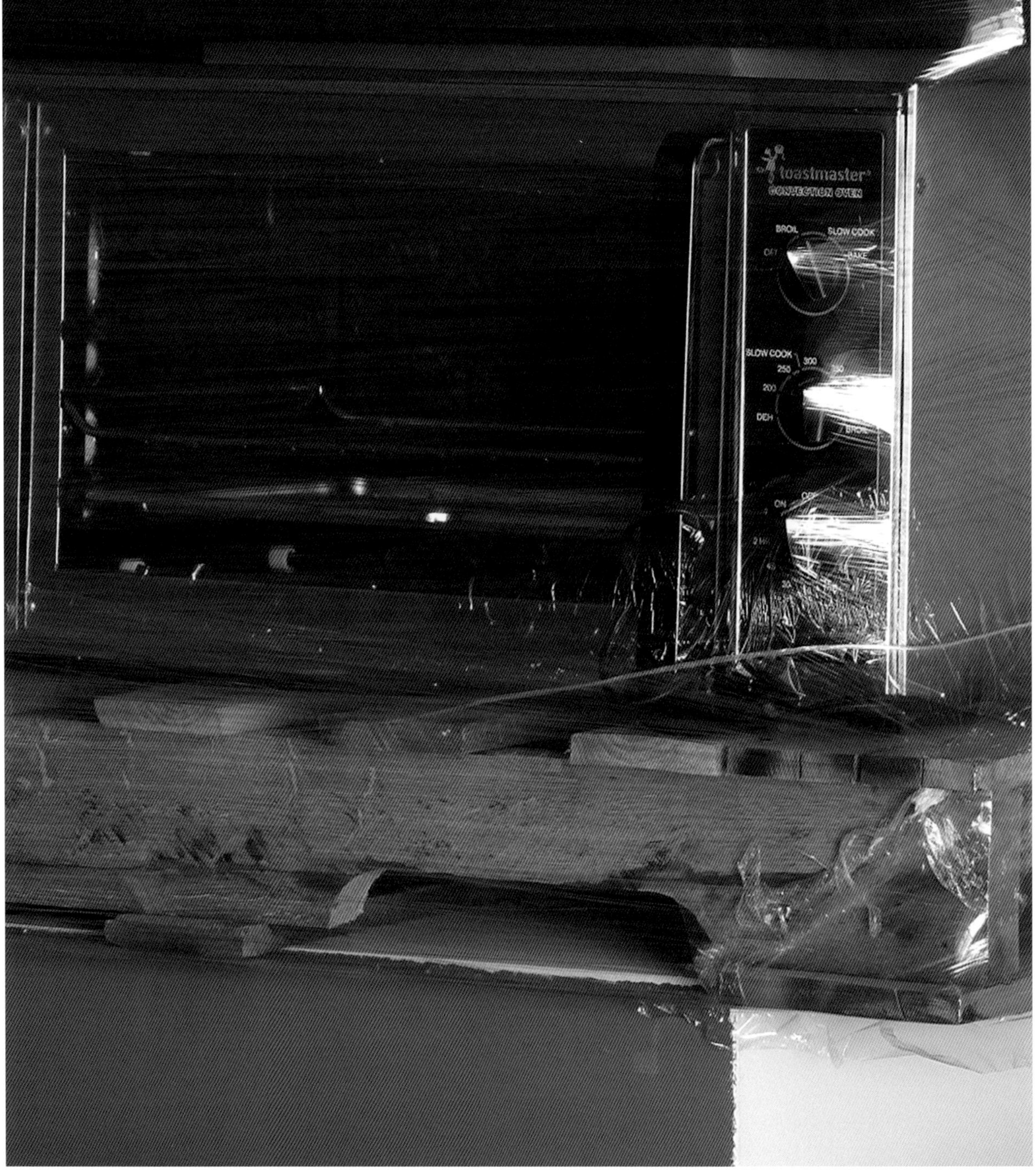

EXCLUSIVE AFFAIR RENTALS
toastmaster
CONVECTION OVEN
BROIL
SLOW COOK
OFF
BAKE
SLOW COOK
300
250
200
DEH
BROIL
ON
2 HR

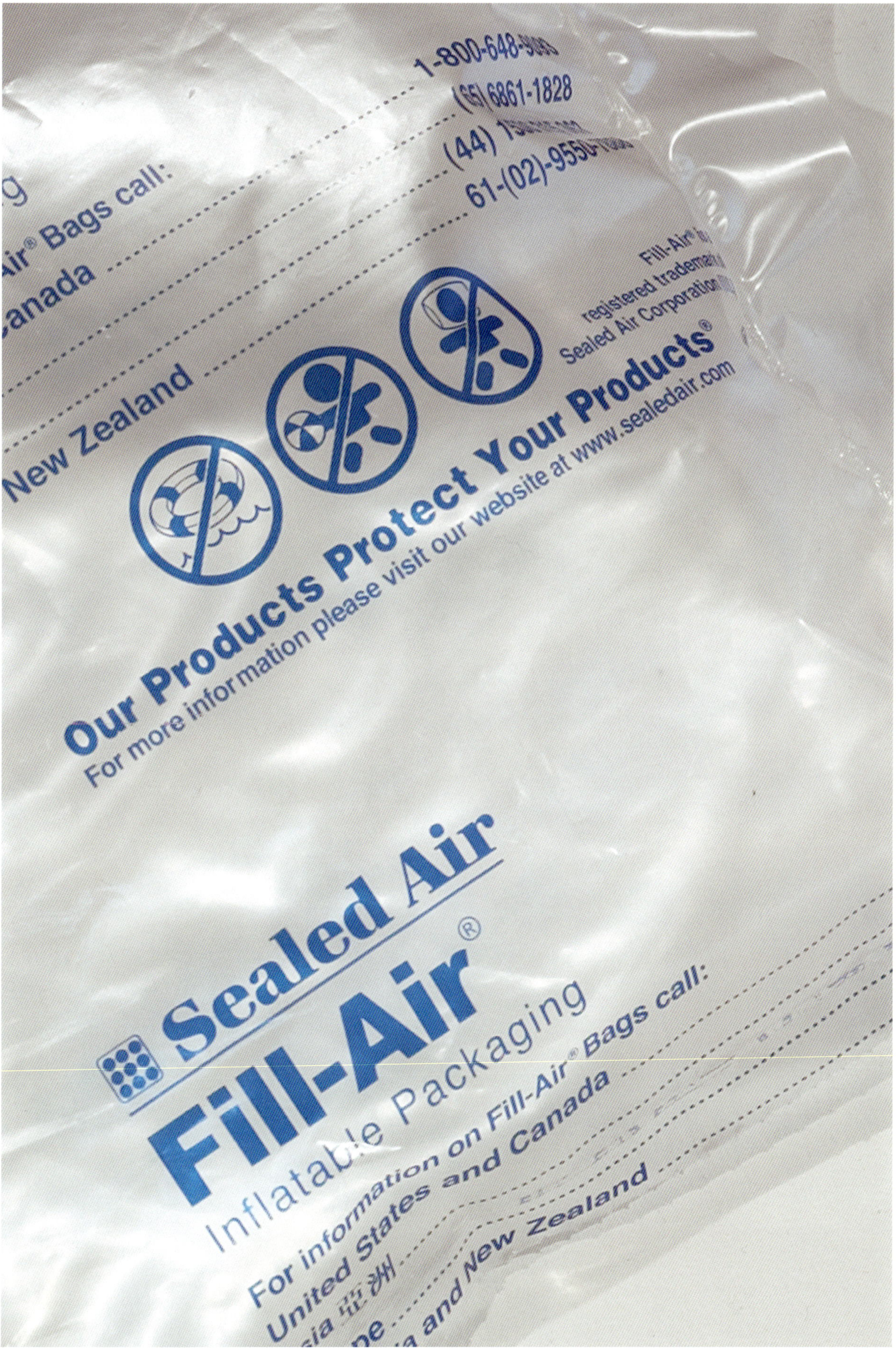

1-800-648-...
(65) 6861-1828
(44) ...
61-(02)-955...

...ir® Bags call:
...anada
New Zealand

Fill-Air is a
registered trademark of
Sealed Air Corporation

Our Products Protect Your Products

For more information please visit our website at www.sealedair.com

Sealed Air
Fill-Air®
Inflatable Packaging

For information on Fill-Air® Bags call:
United States and Canada
...and New Zealand

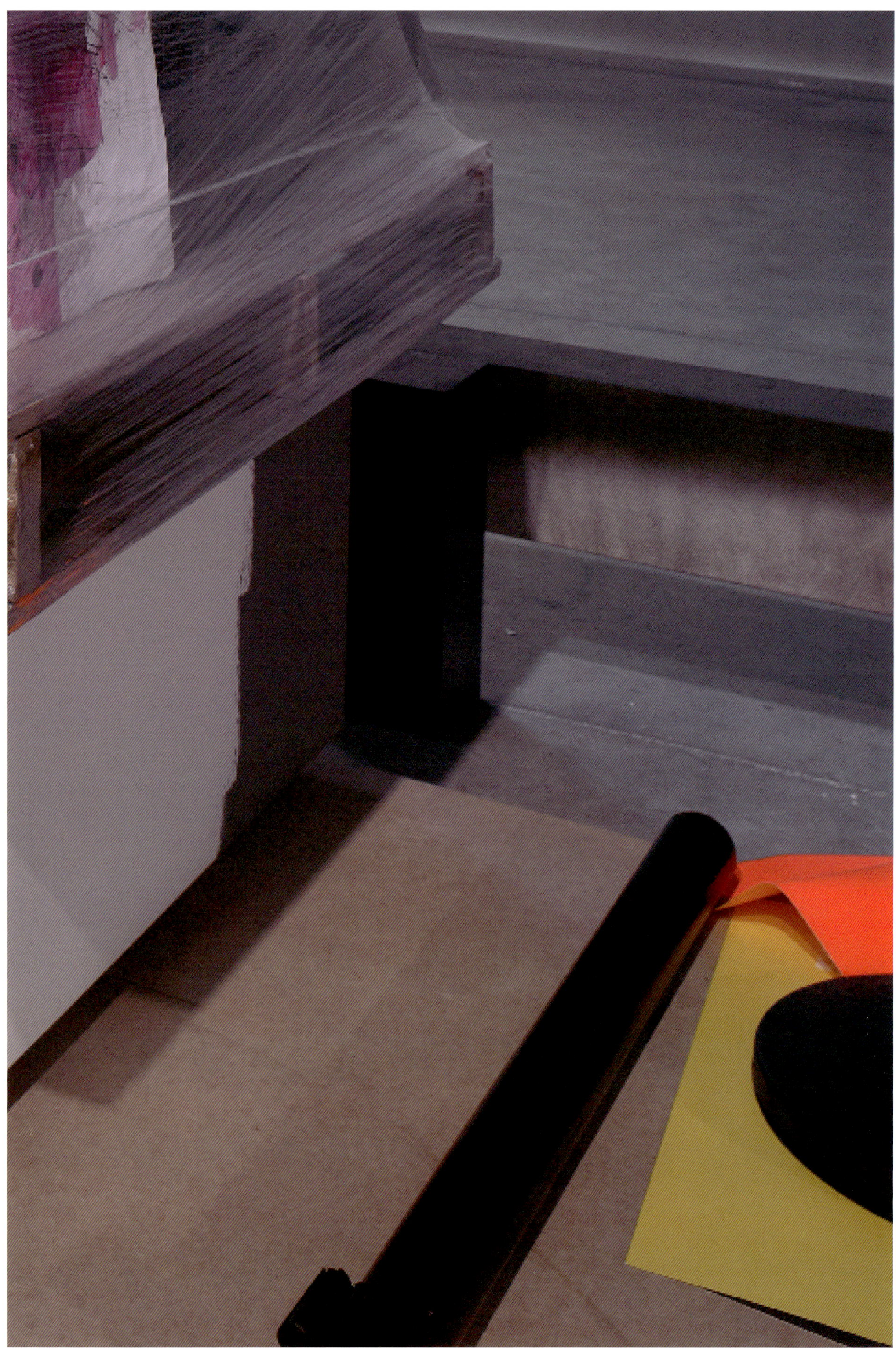

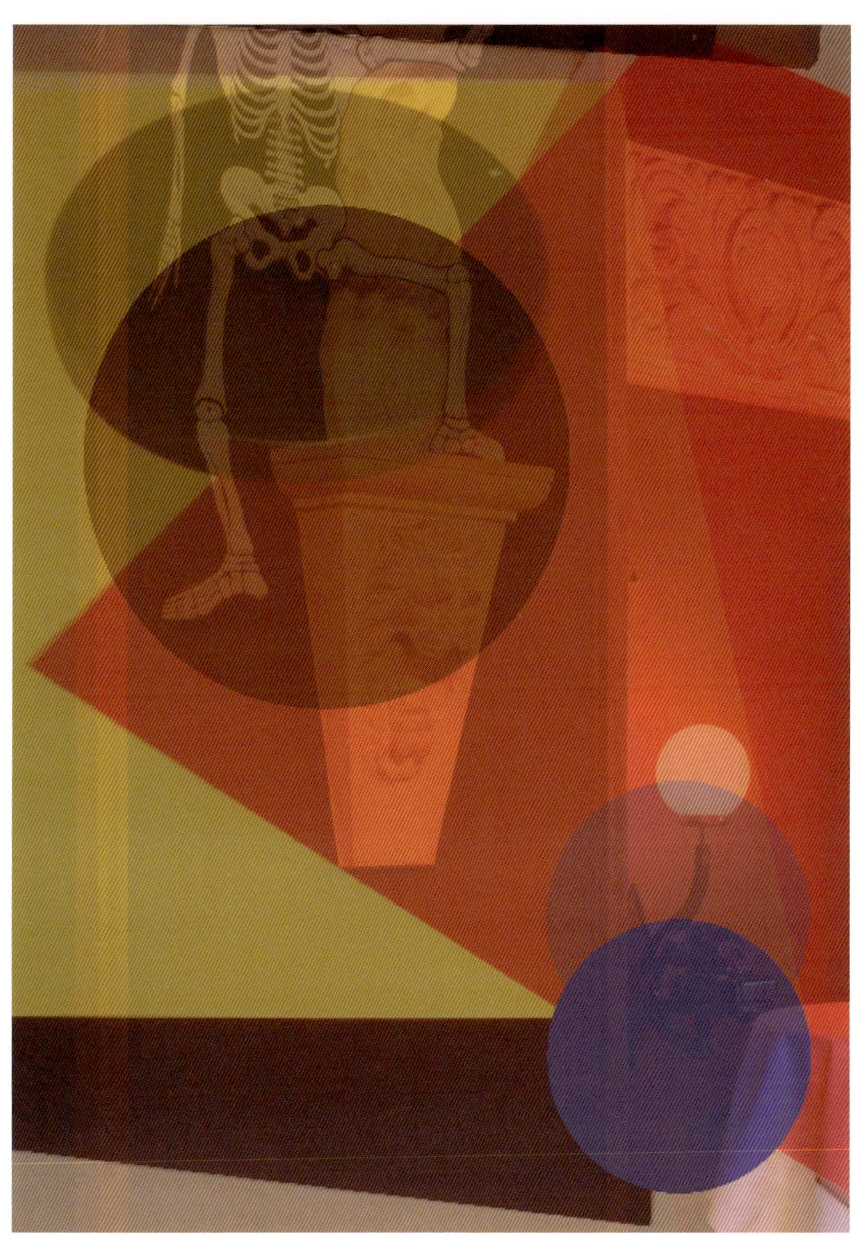

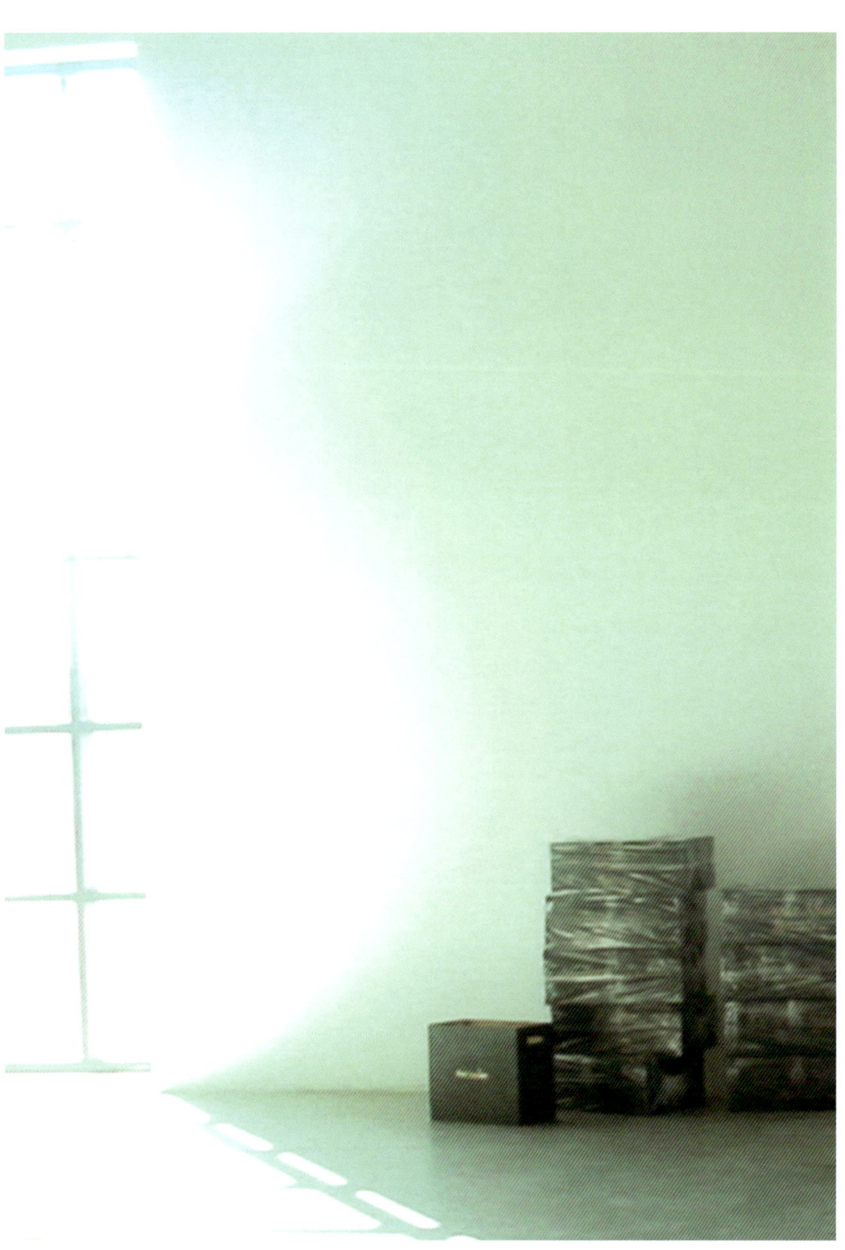

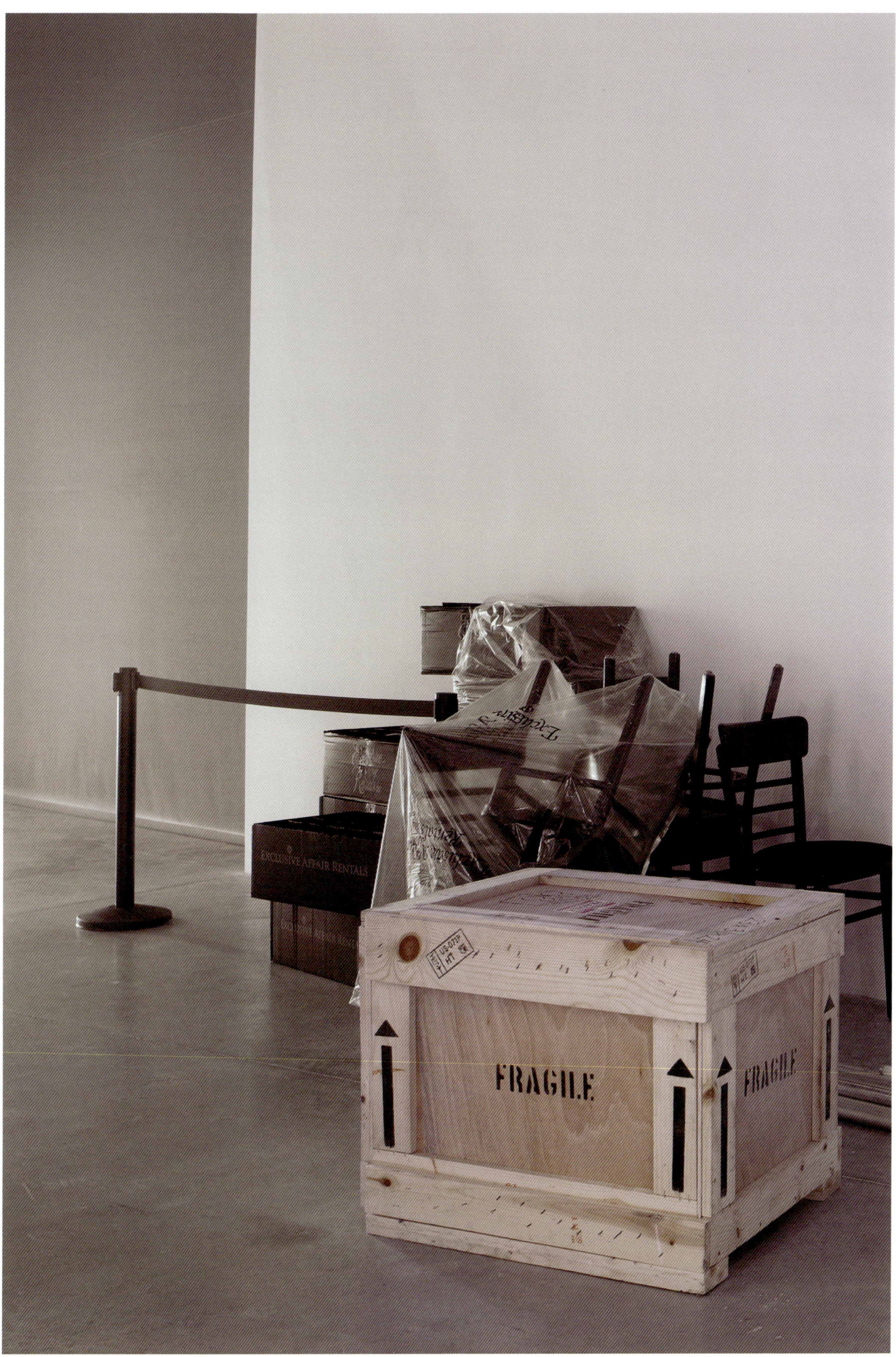
EXCLUSIVE AFFAIR RENTALS
FRAGILE
FRAGILE

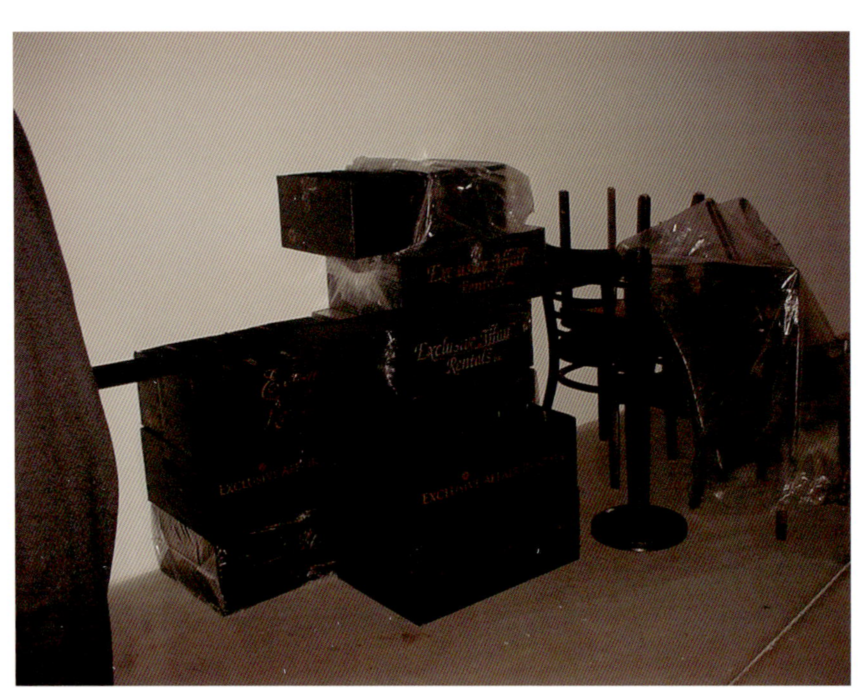

Exclusive Affair Rentals inc.
Exclusive Affair Rentals inc.
EXCLUSIVE AFFAIR RENTALS

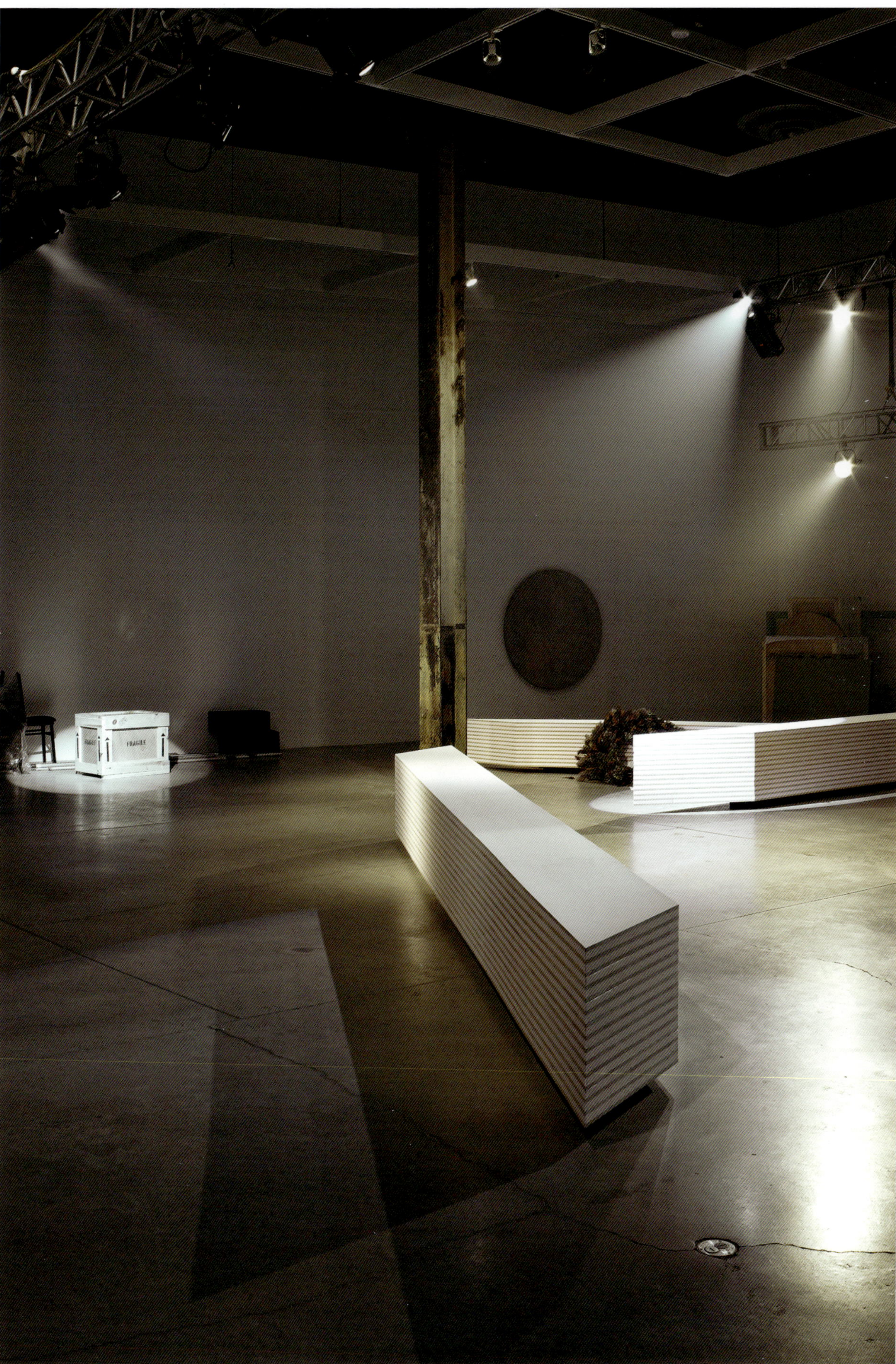

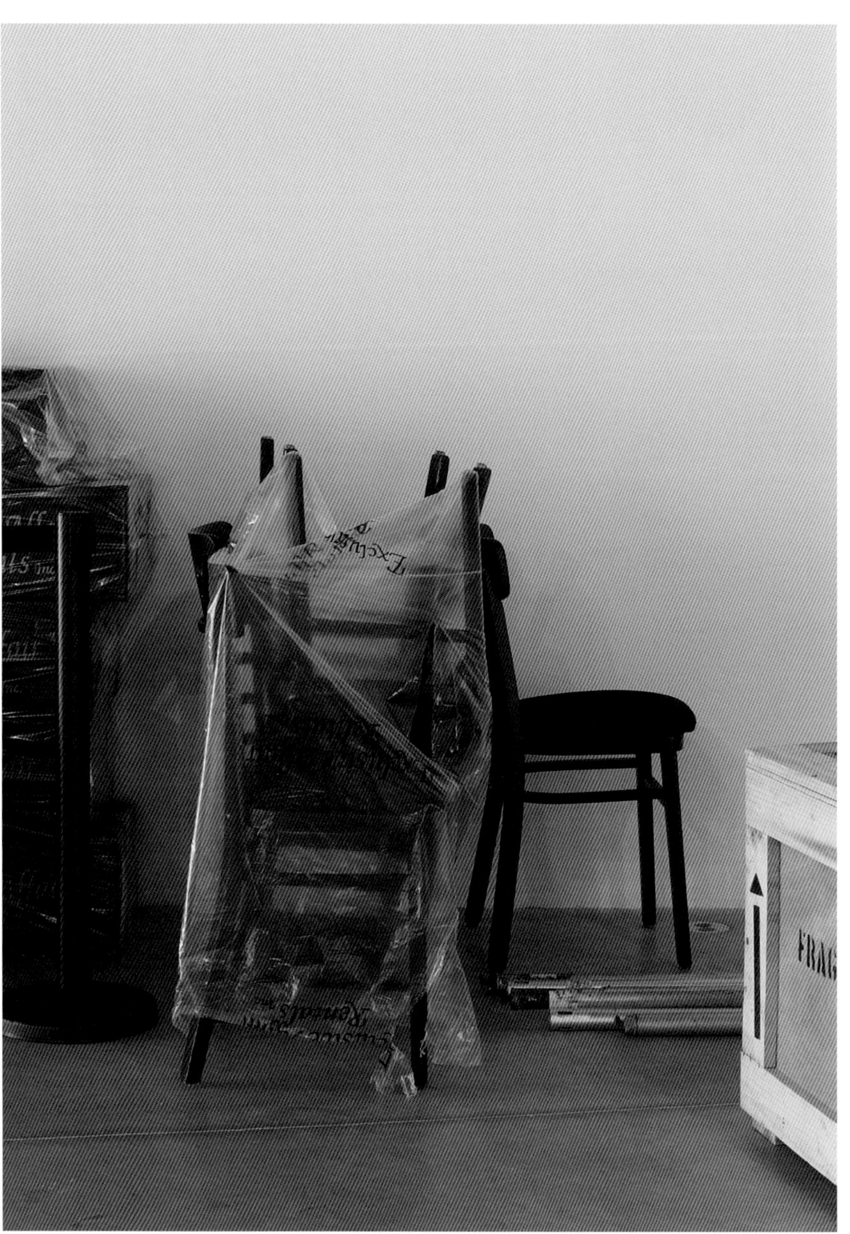

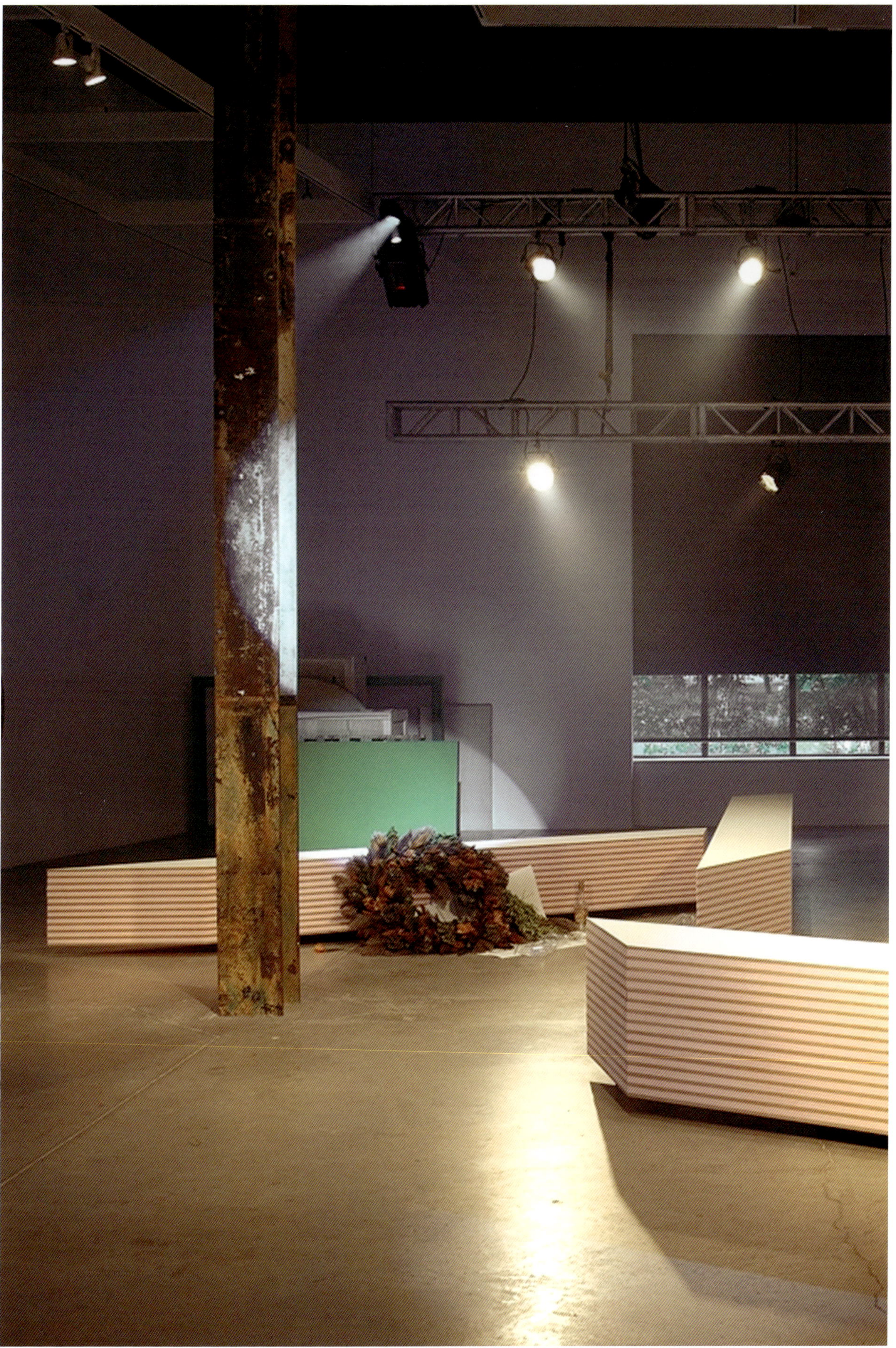

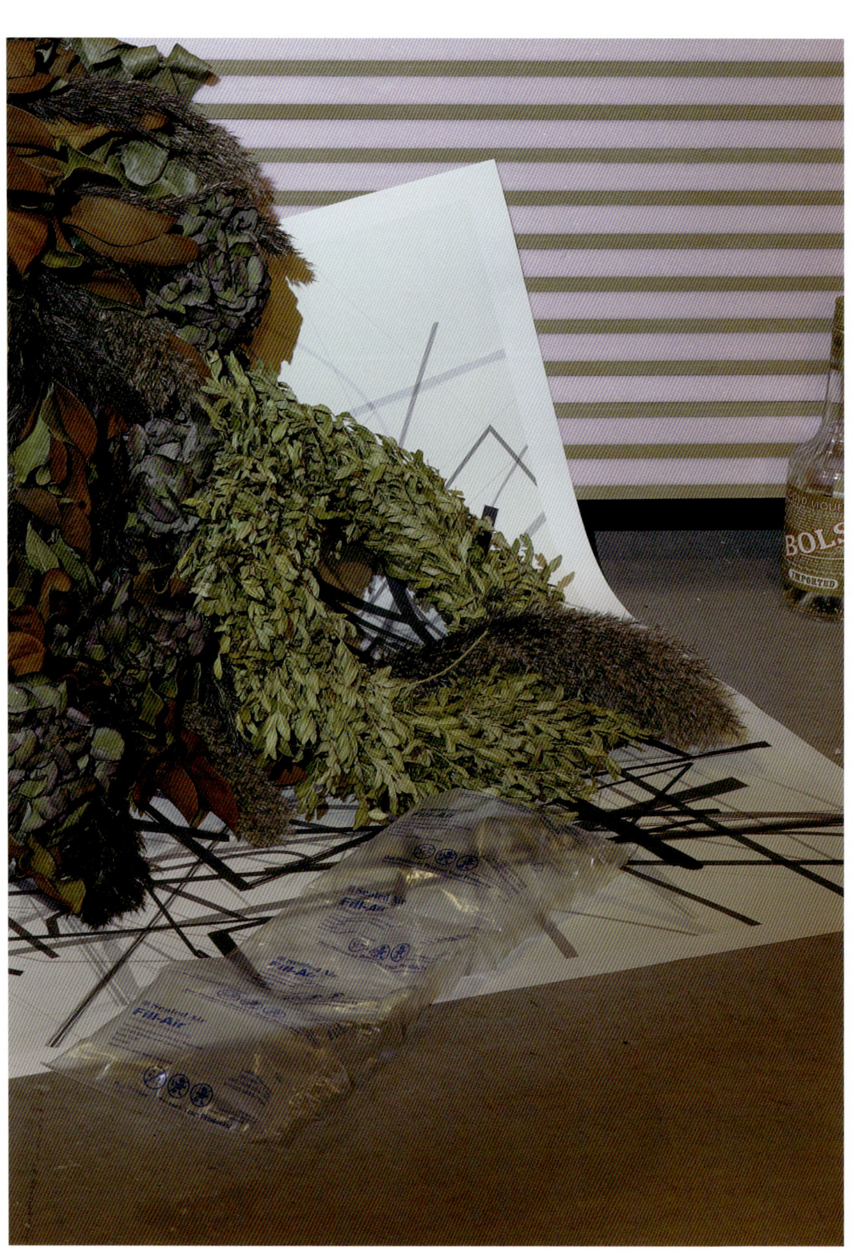

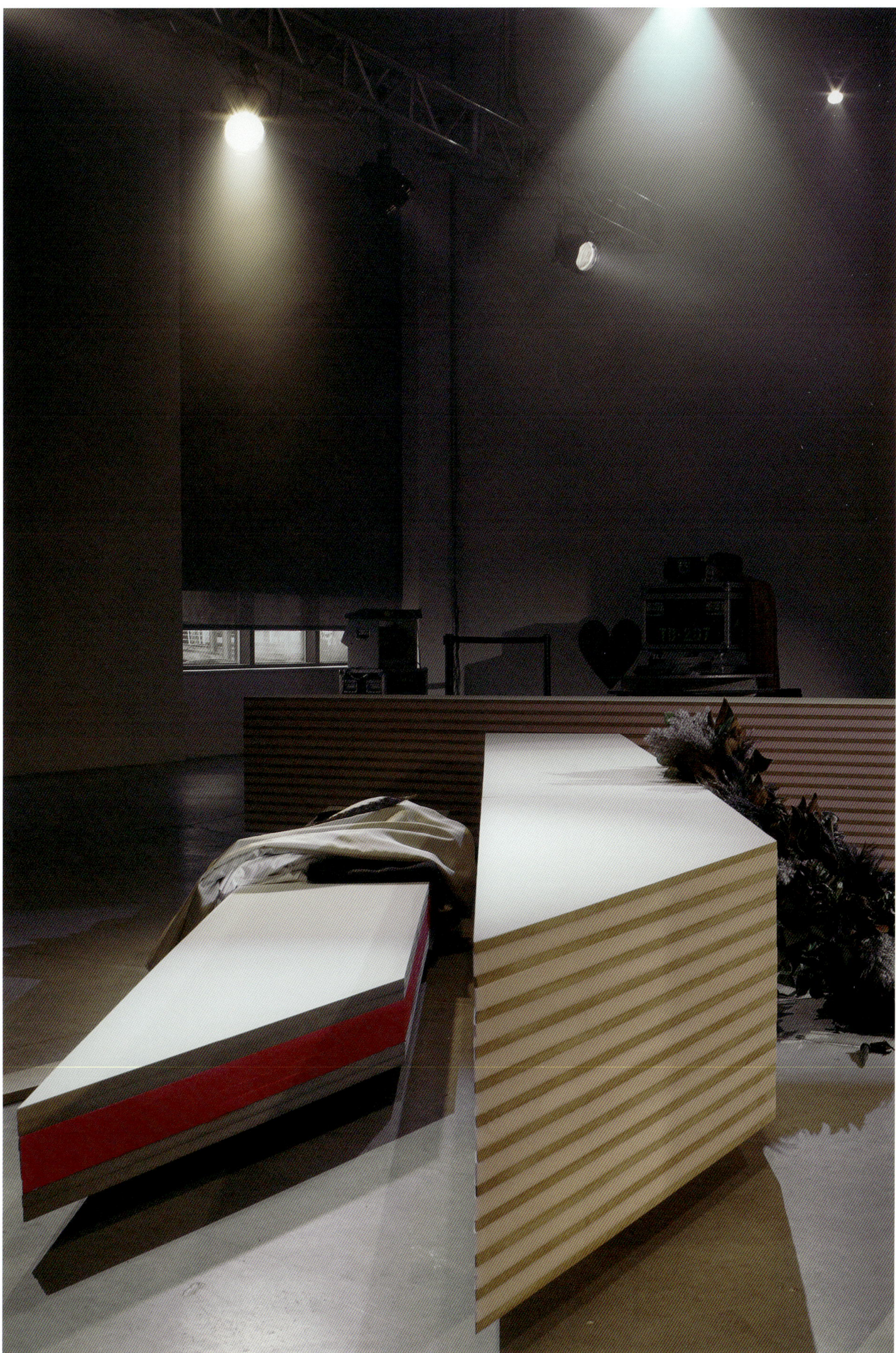

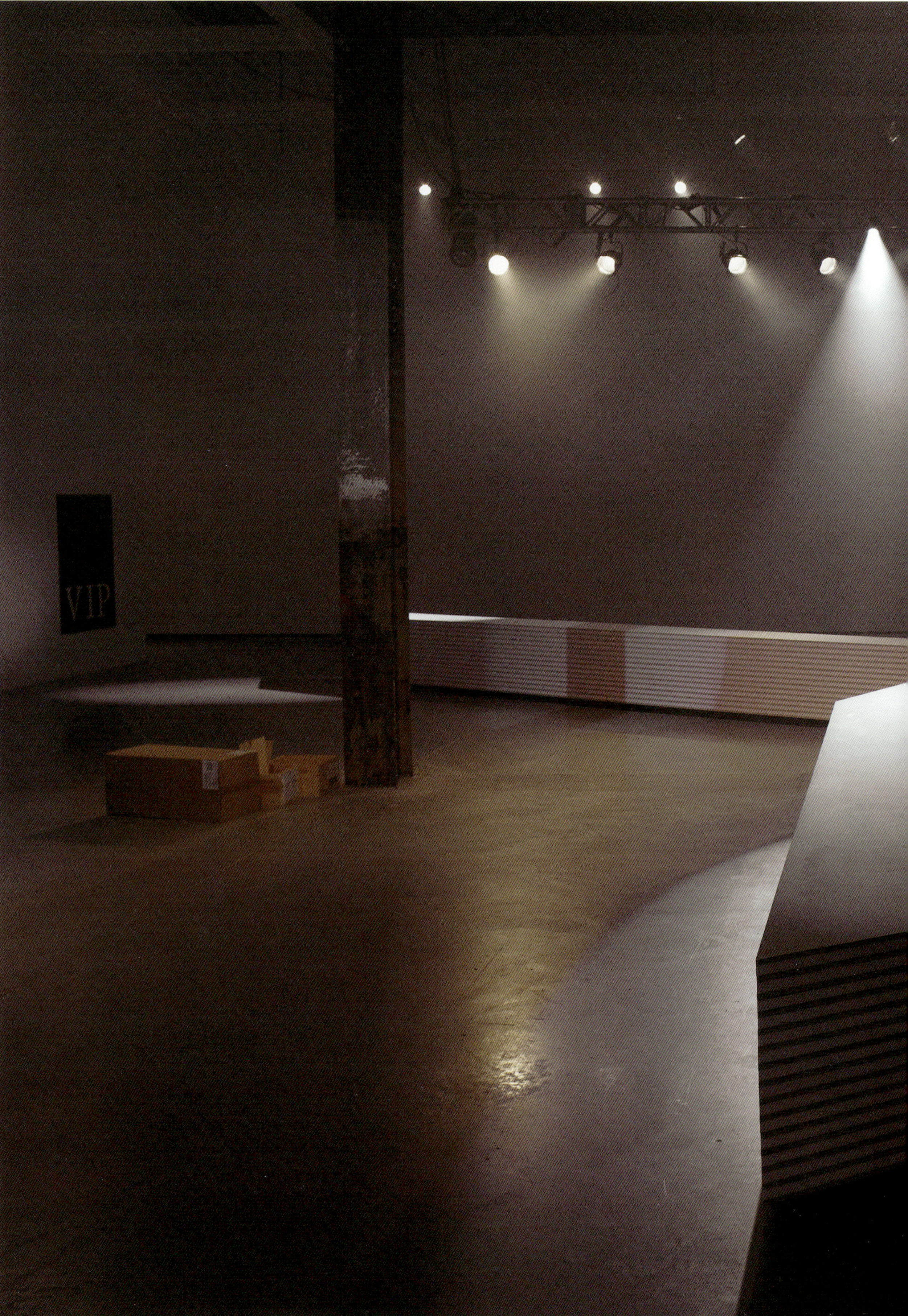

VIP

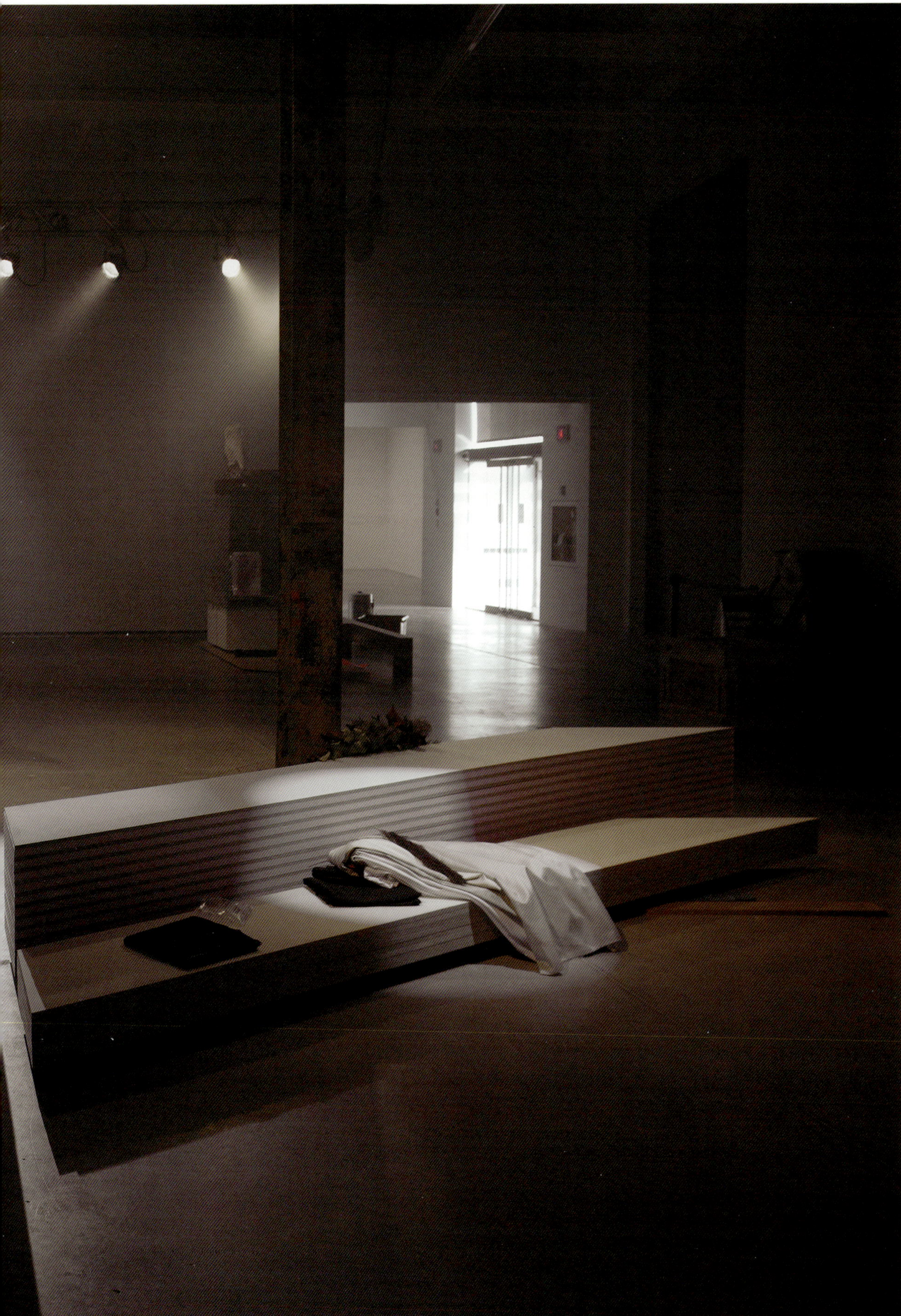

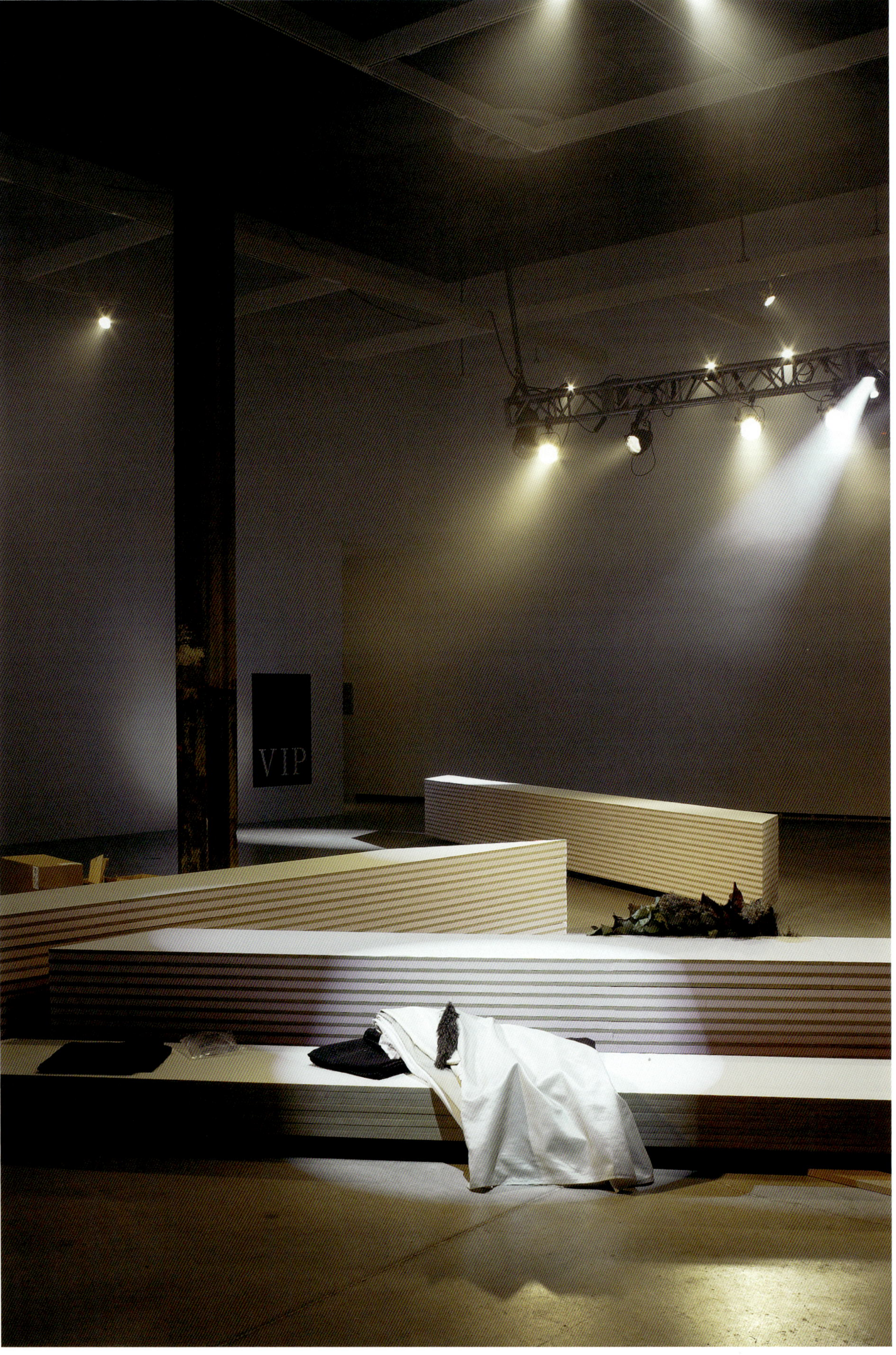

VIP

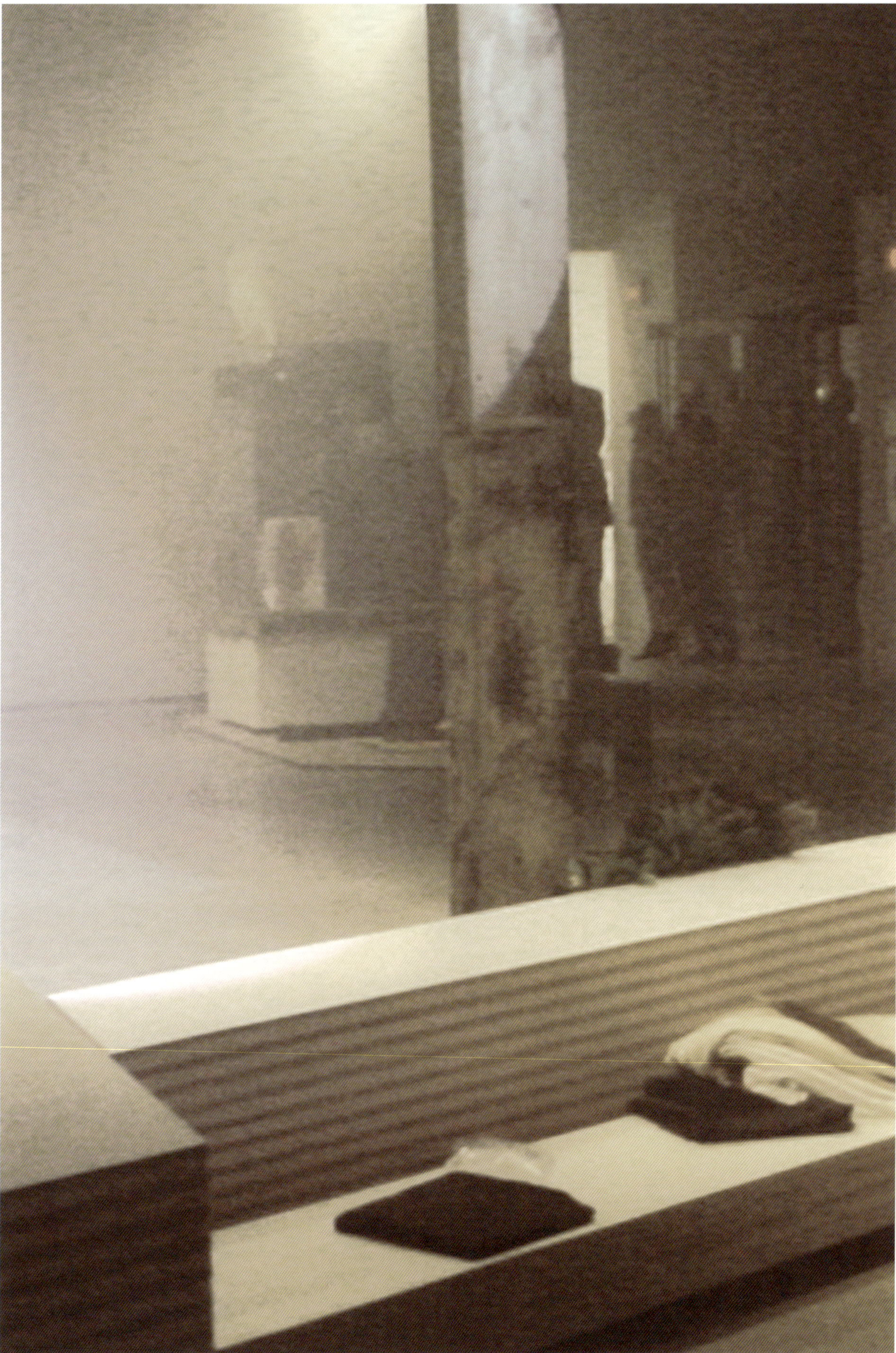

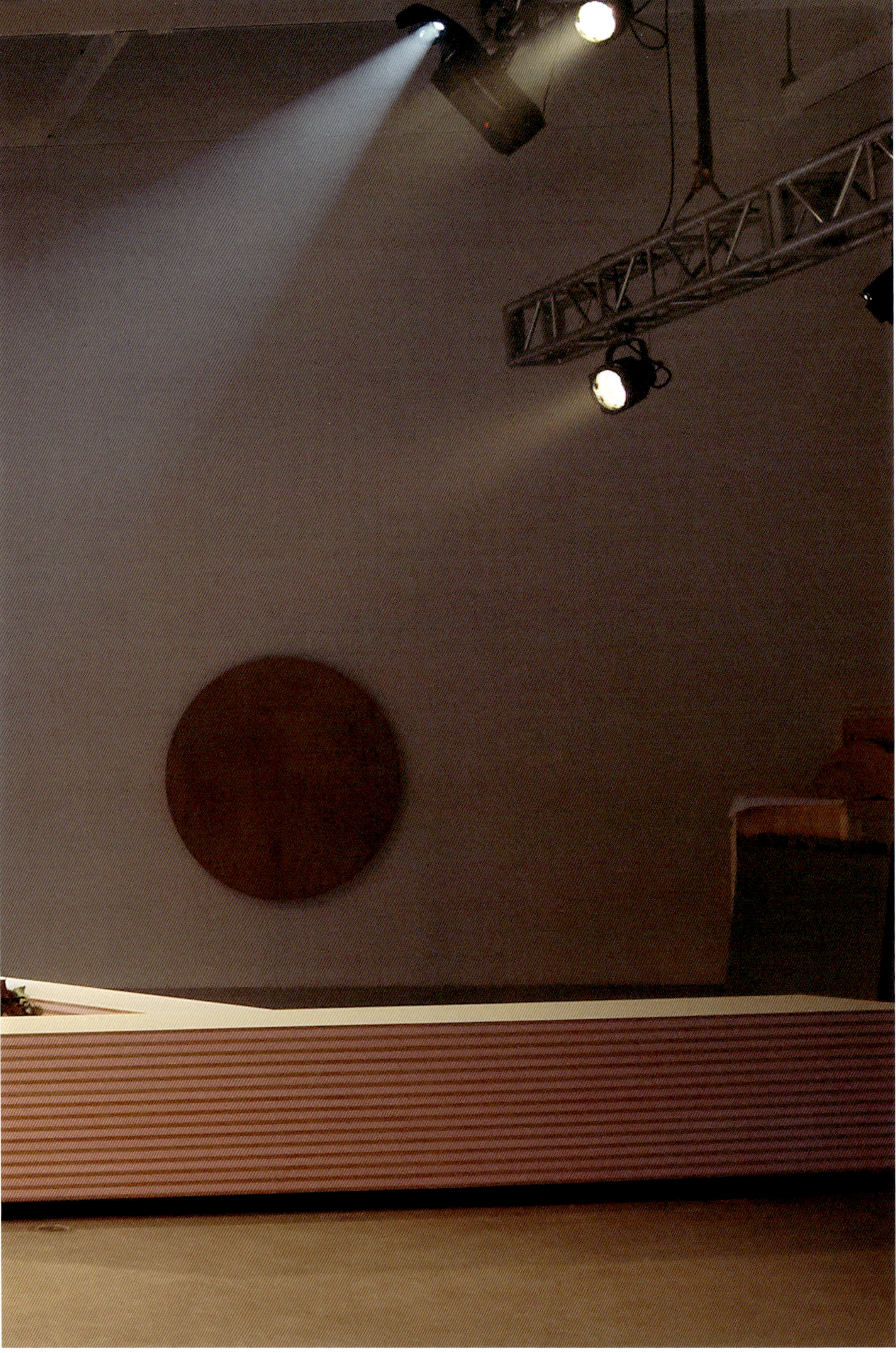

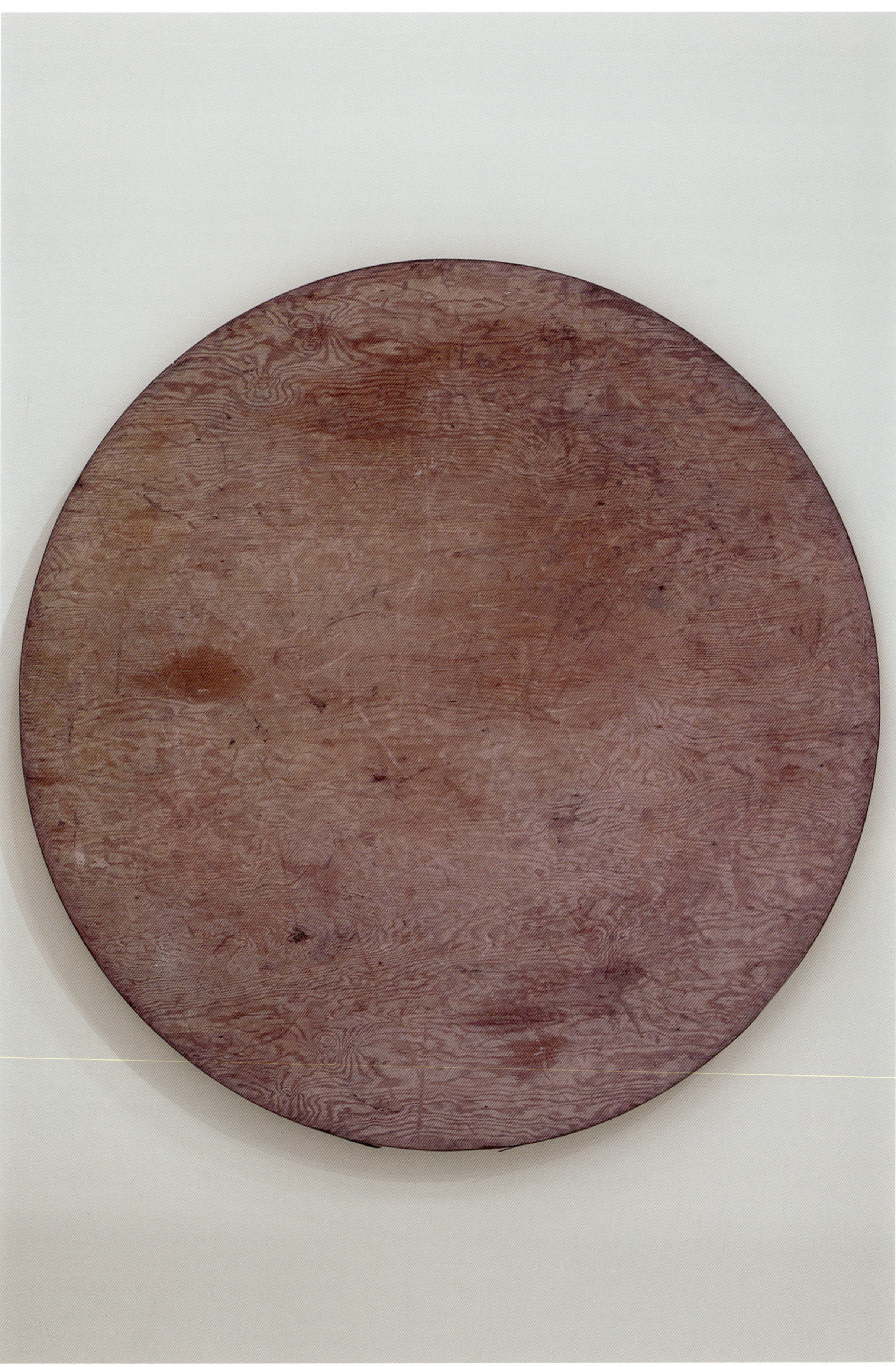

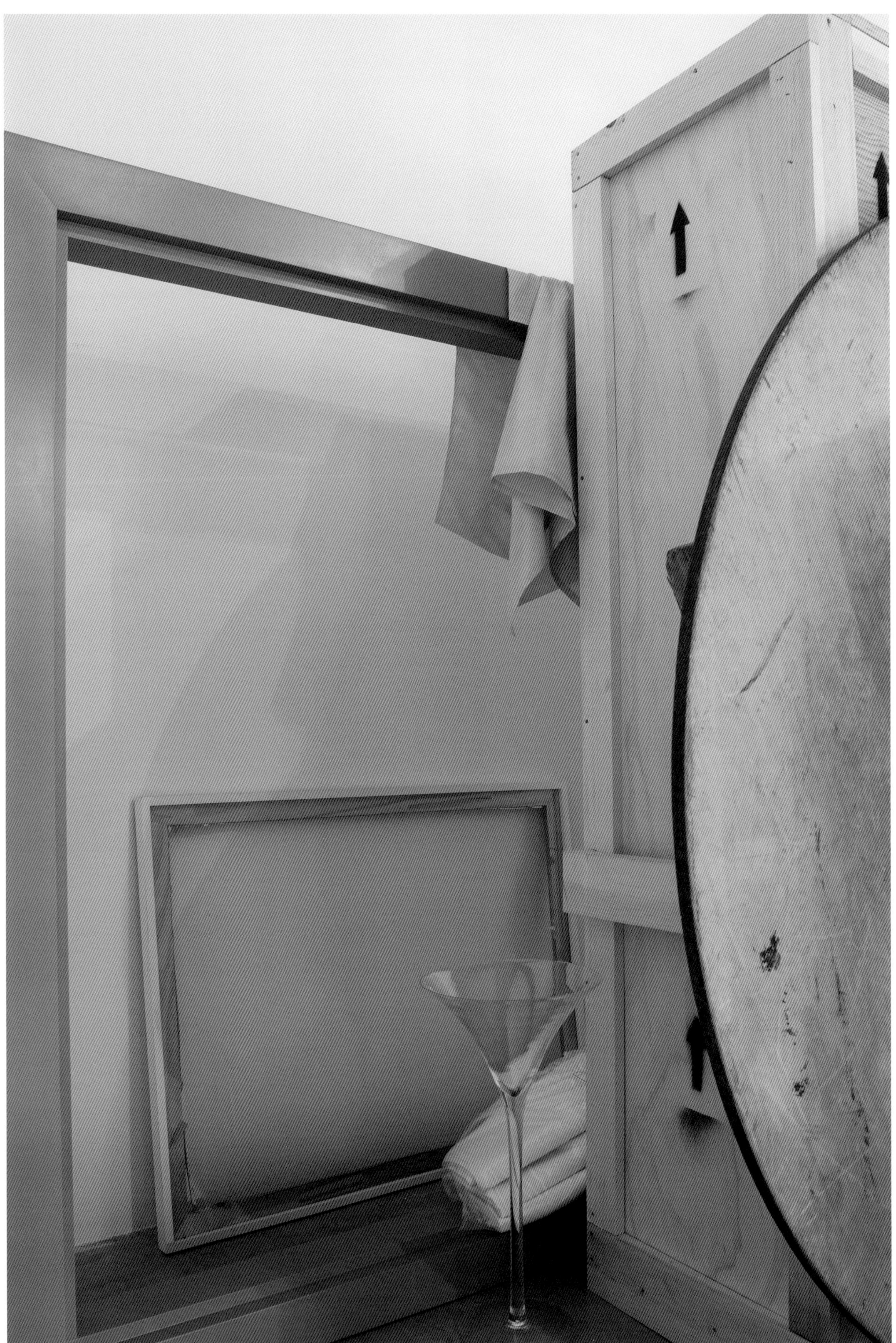

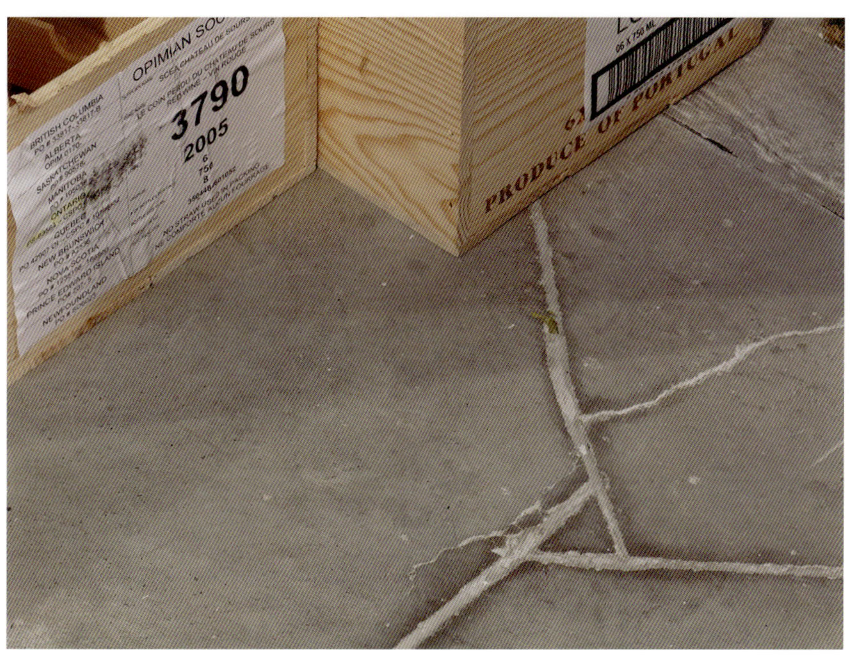

OPIMIAN SO...
SCEA CHATEAU DE SOURS
LE COIN PERDU DU CHATEAU DE SOURS
RED WINE – VIN ROUGE
3790
2005
6
75¢
8
NO STRAW USED IN PACKING
NE COMPORTE AUCUN FOURRAGE
BRITISH COLUMBIA
PO # 33817-33817-6
ALBERTA
OPIM 0170-
SASKATCHEWAN
PO # 90576-
MANITOBA
PO # 1050
ONTARIO
QUEBEC
PO 42907 01 – CSPC #
NEW BRUNSWICK
PO # A7376
NOVA SCOTIA
PRINCE EDWARD ISLAND
NEWFOUNDLAND
06 X 750 ML
PRODUCE OF PORTUGAL

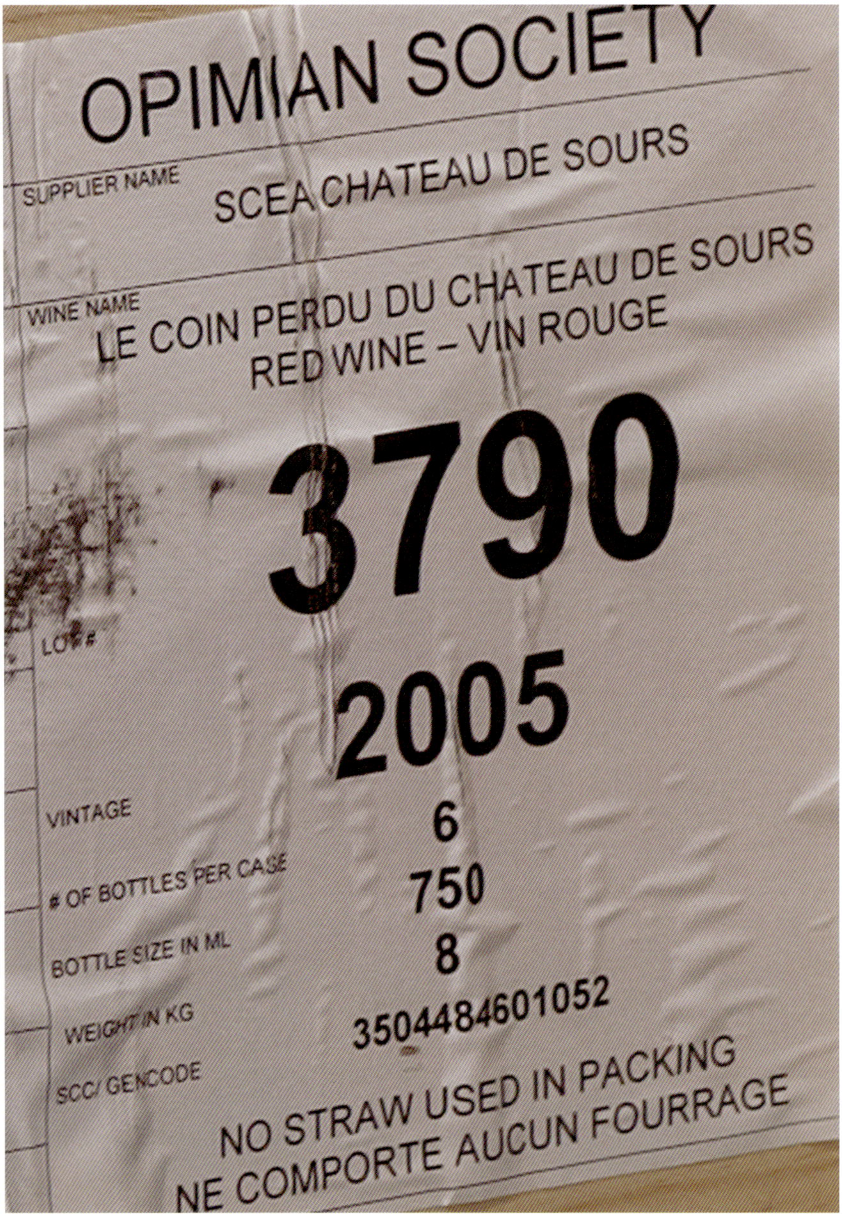

OPIMIAN SOCIETY

SUPPLIER NAME   SCEA CHATEAU DE SOURS

WINE NAME   LE COIN PERDU DU CHATEAU DE SOURS
RED WINE – VIN ROUGE

3790

2005

LOT #

VINTAGE   6

OF BOTTLES PER CASE   750

BOTTLE SIZE IN ML   8

WEIGHT IN KG   3504484601052

SCC/ GENCODE

NO STRAW USED IN PACKING
NE COMPORTE AUCUN FOURRAGE

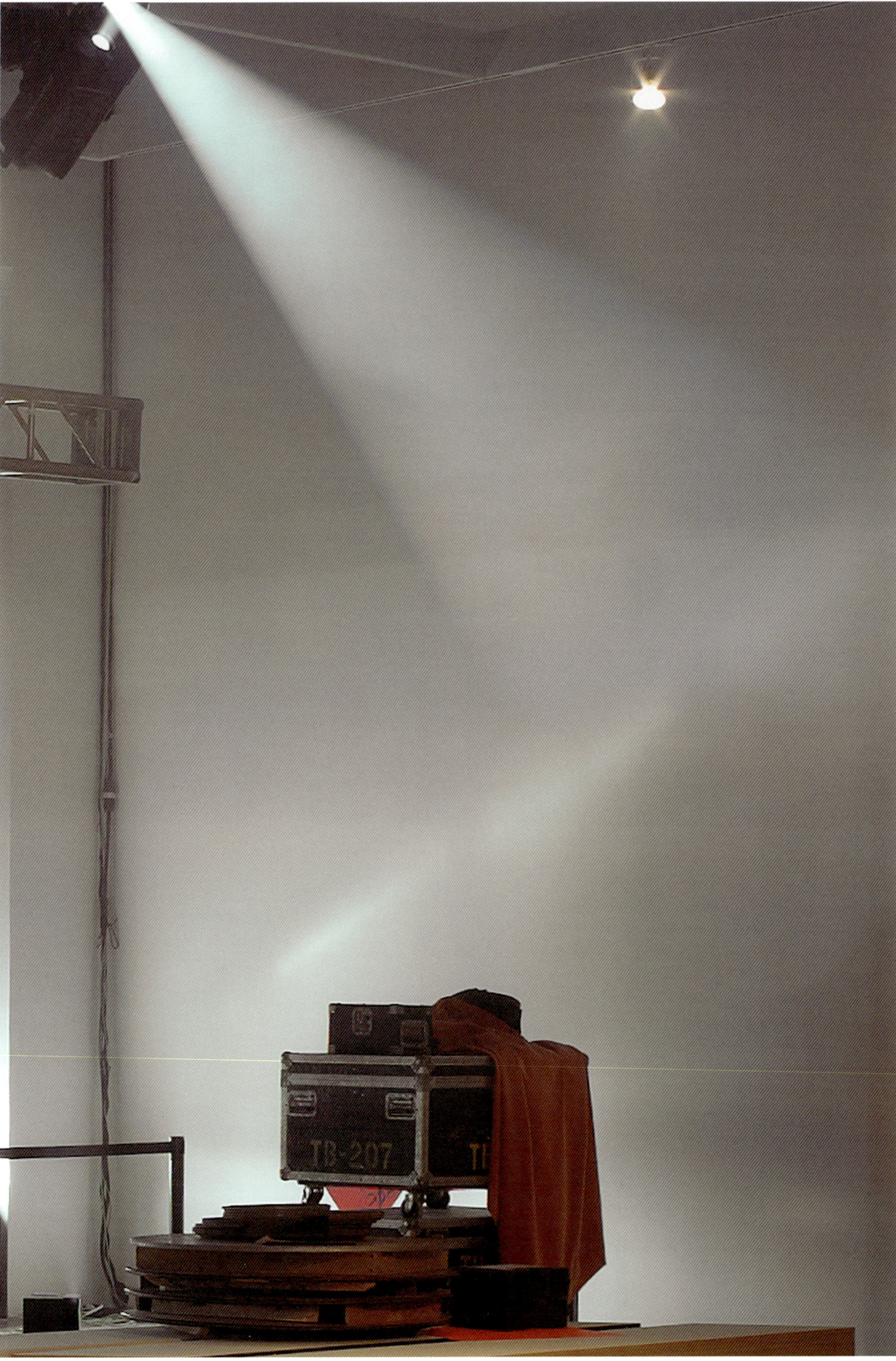

TB-207
TB

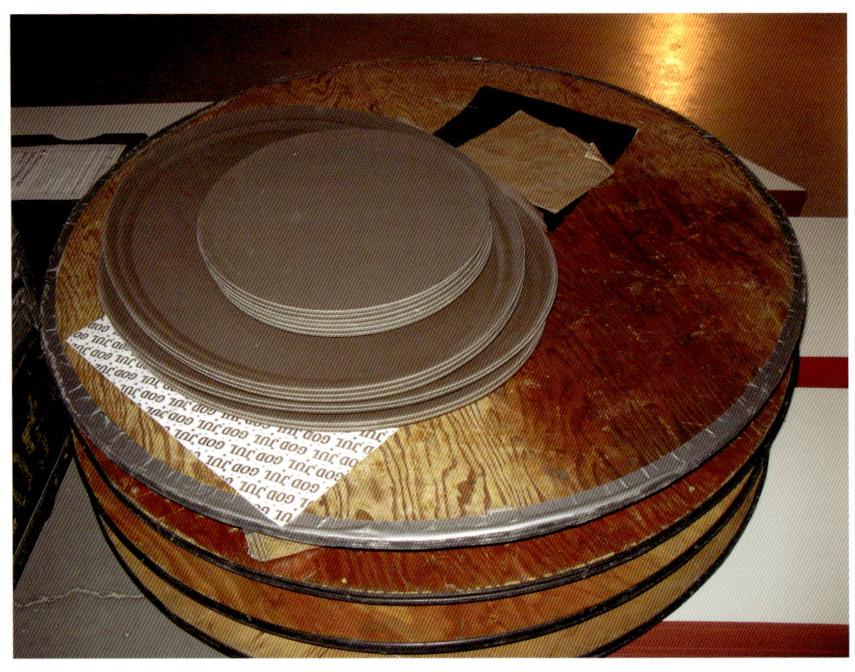
GOD JUL

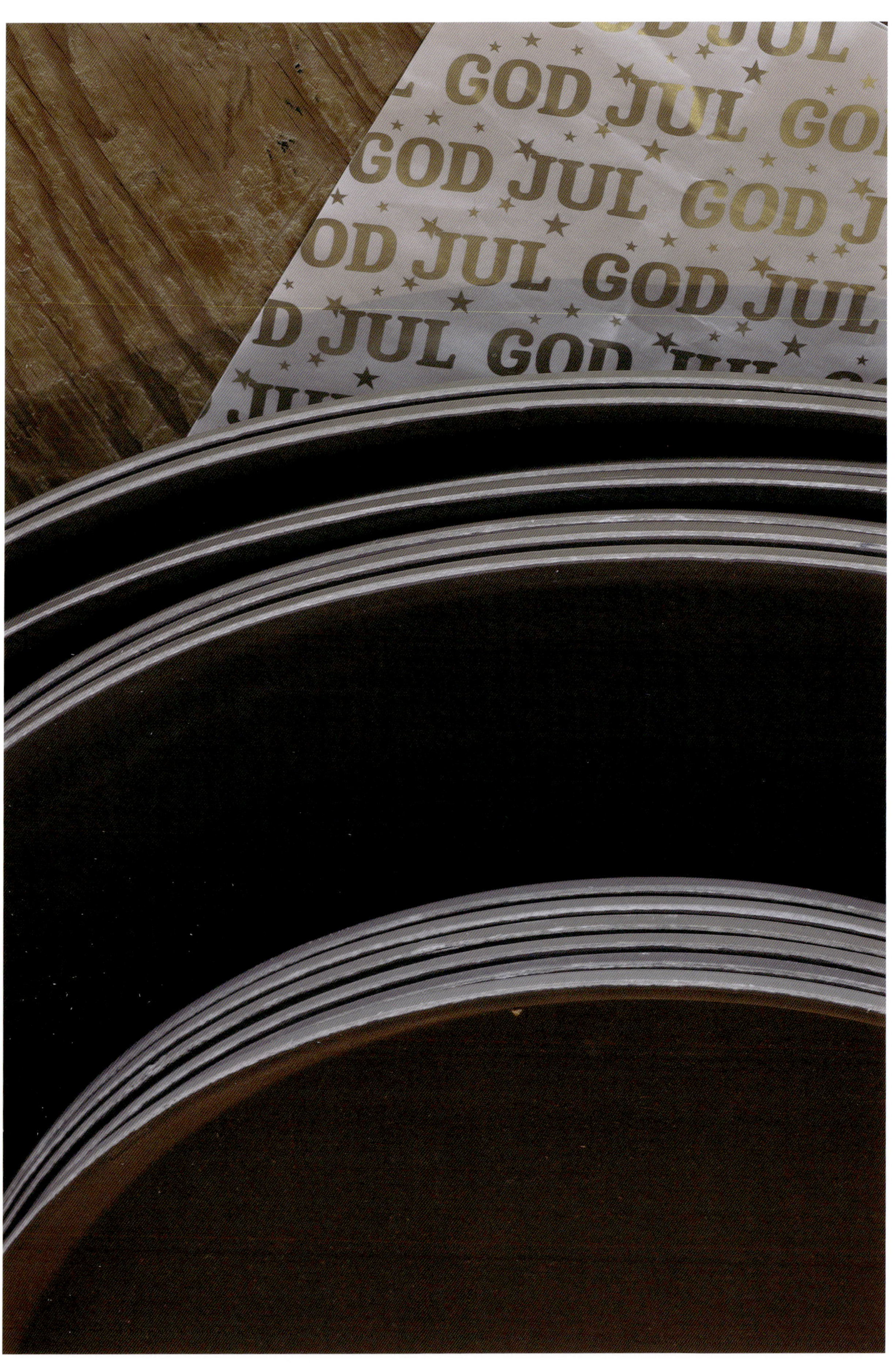
GOD JUL GOD
GOD JUL GOD J
OD JUL GOD JUL
D JUL GOD JUL

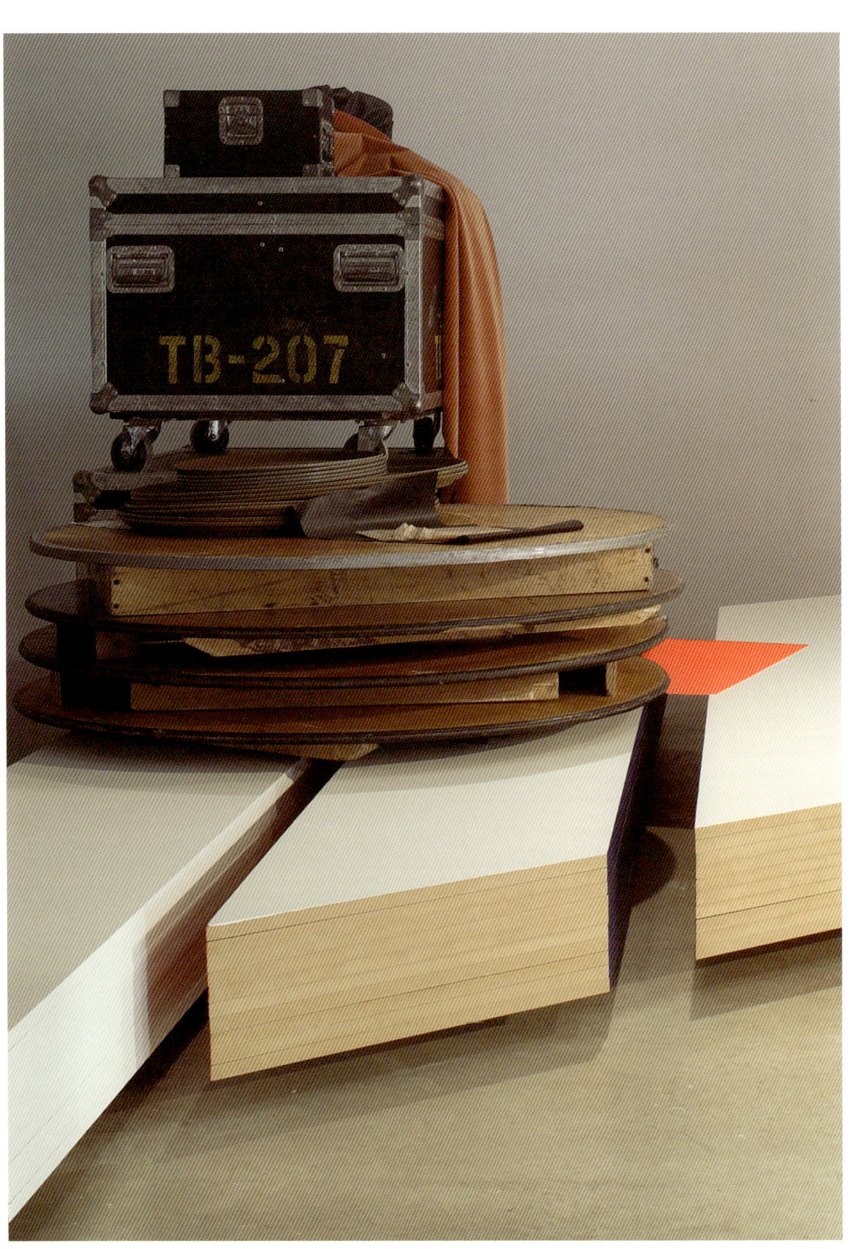
TB-207

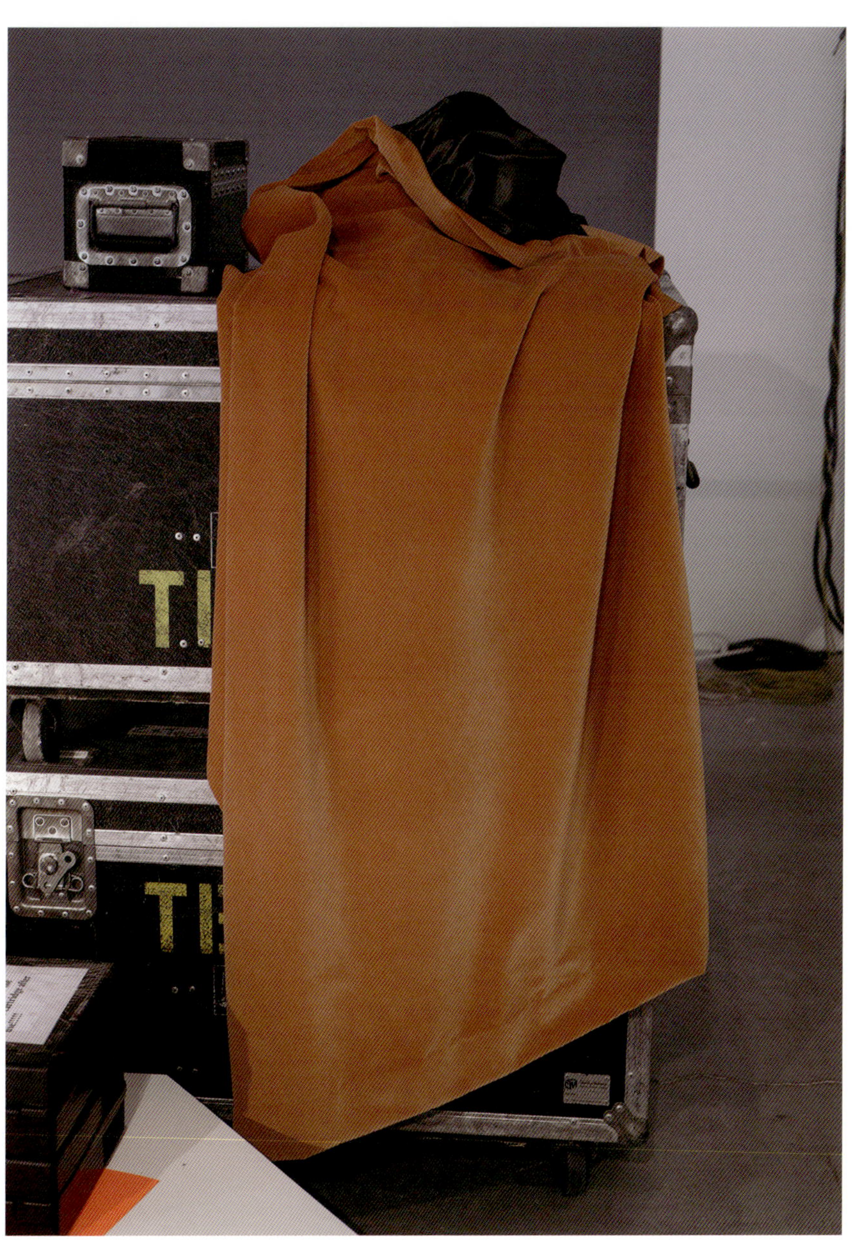

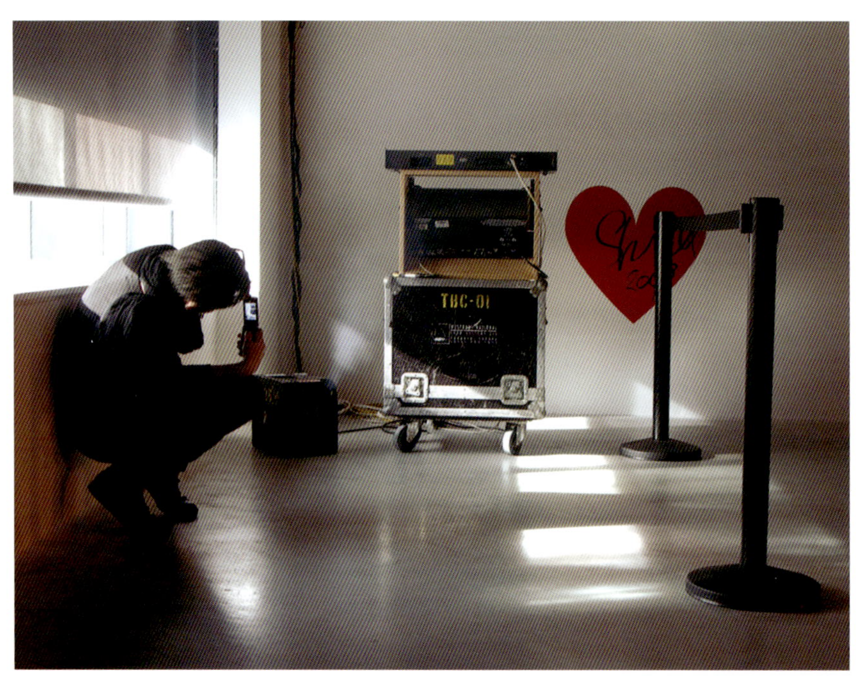

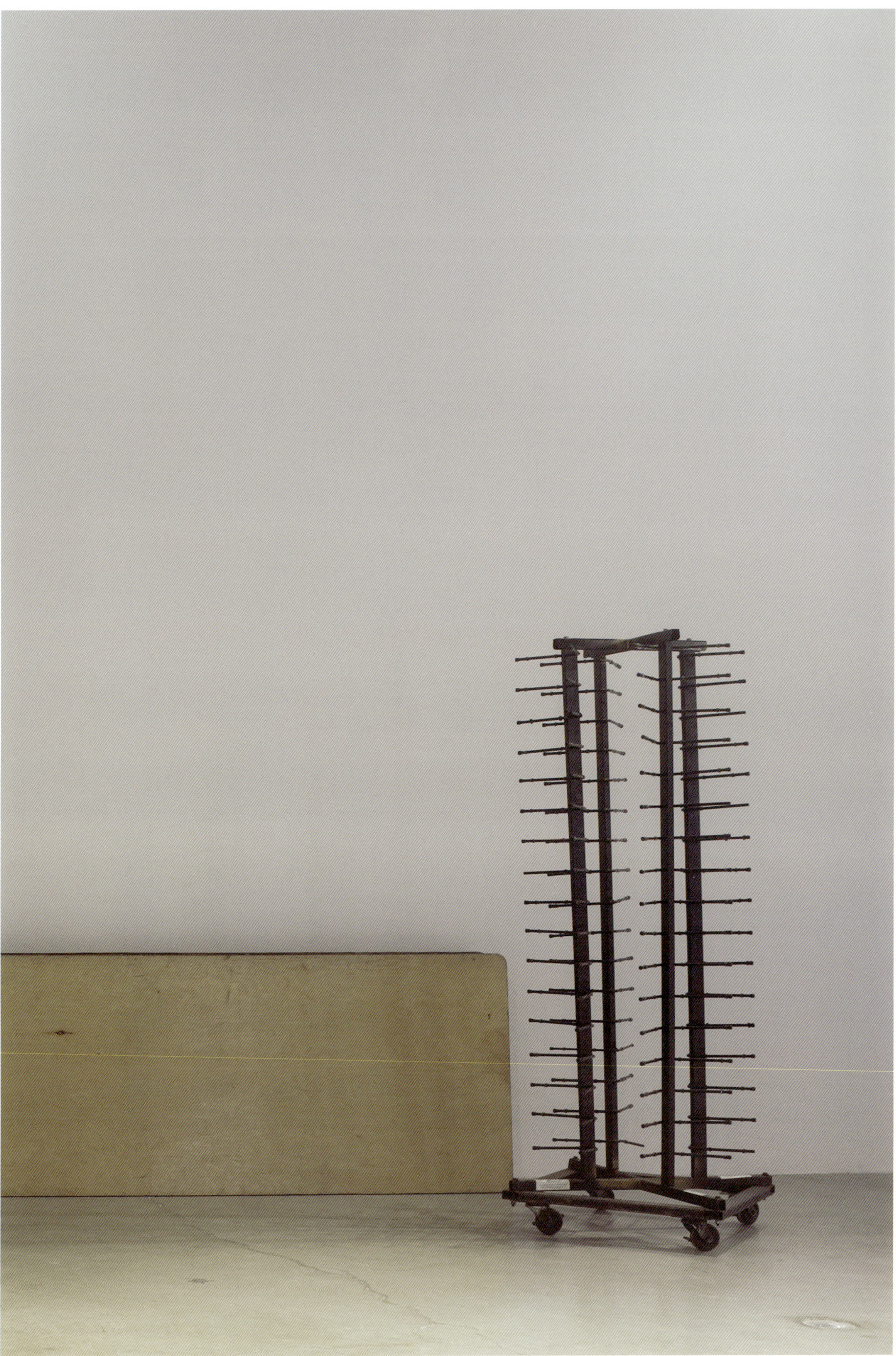

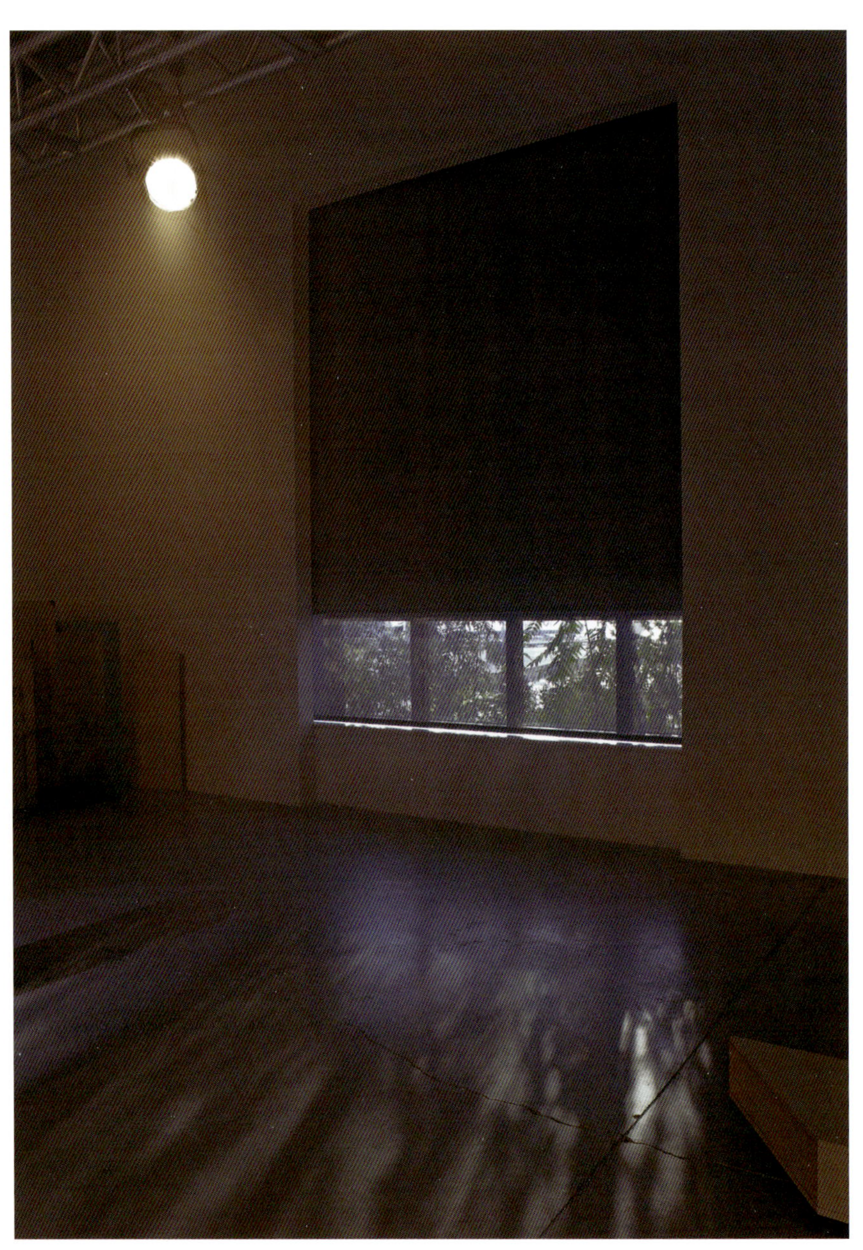

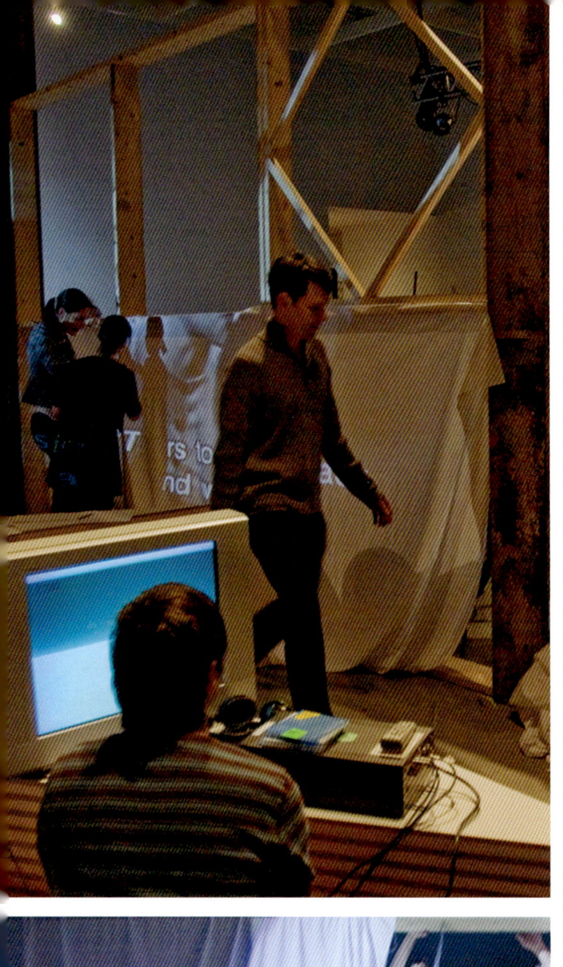
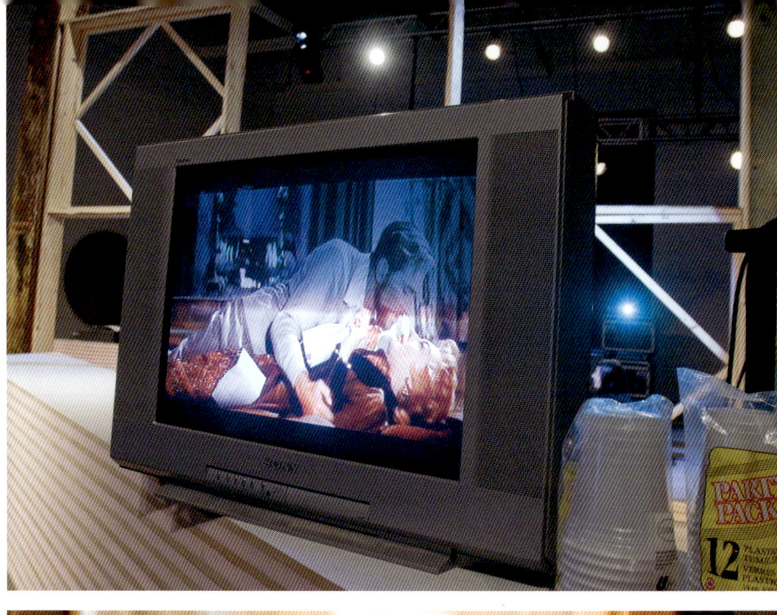
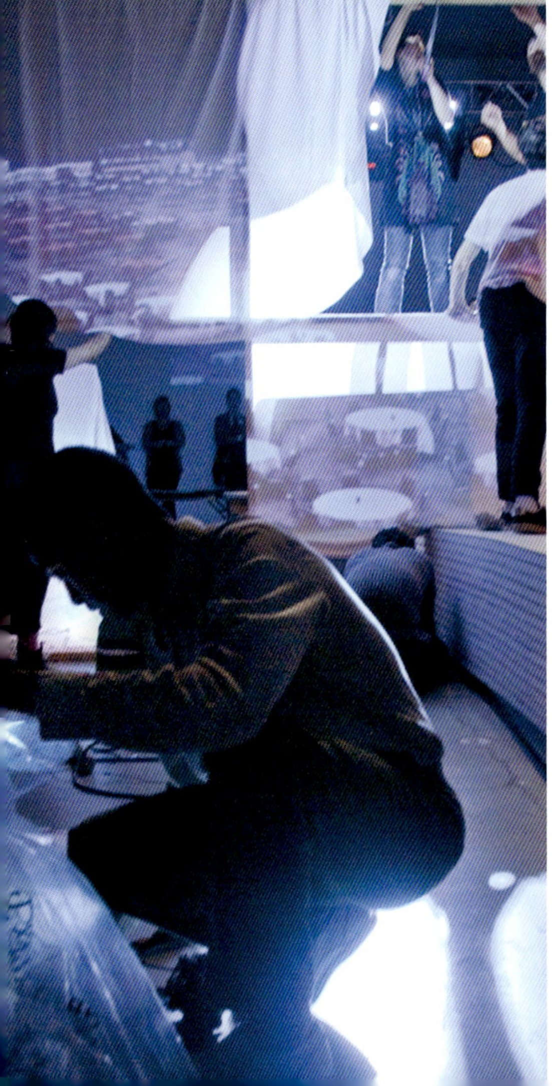

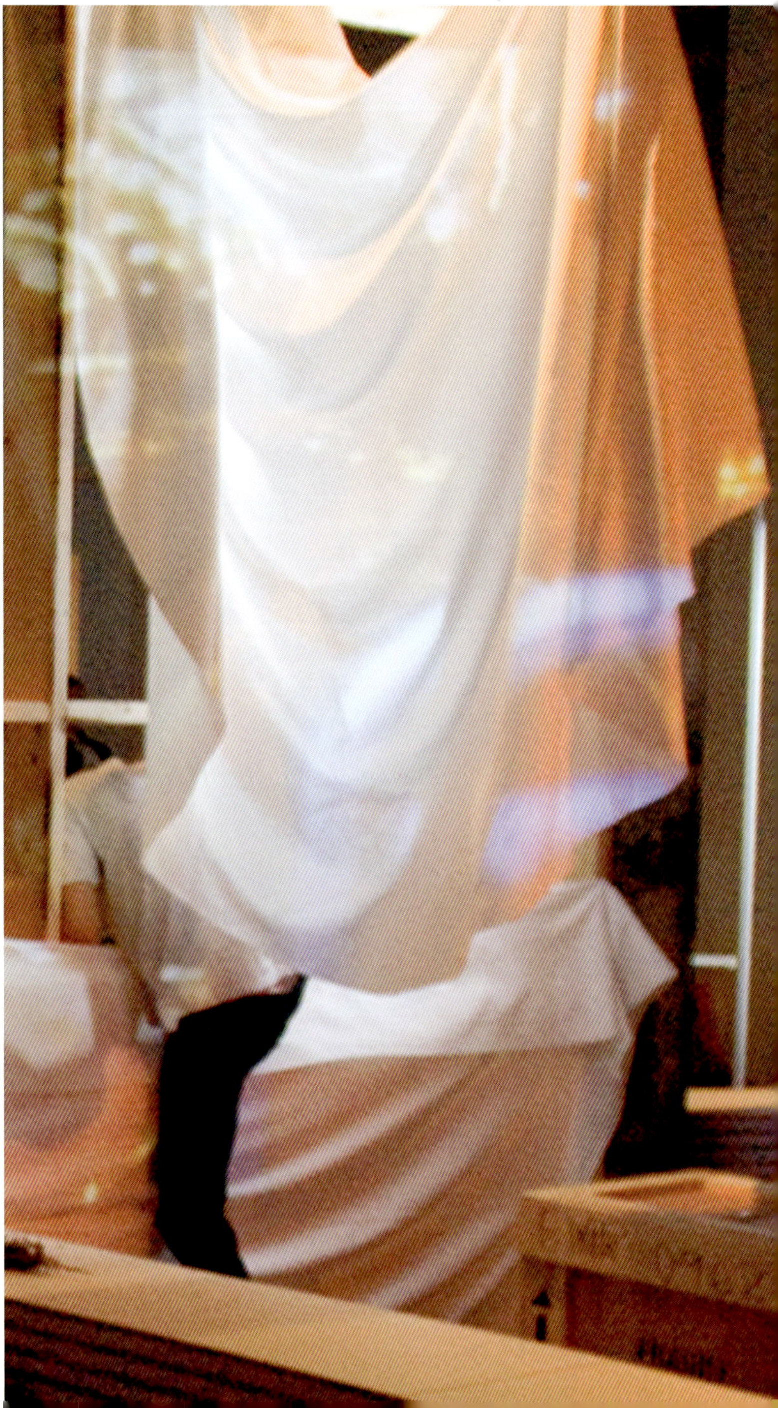

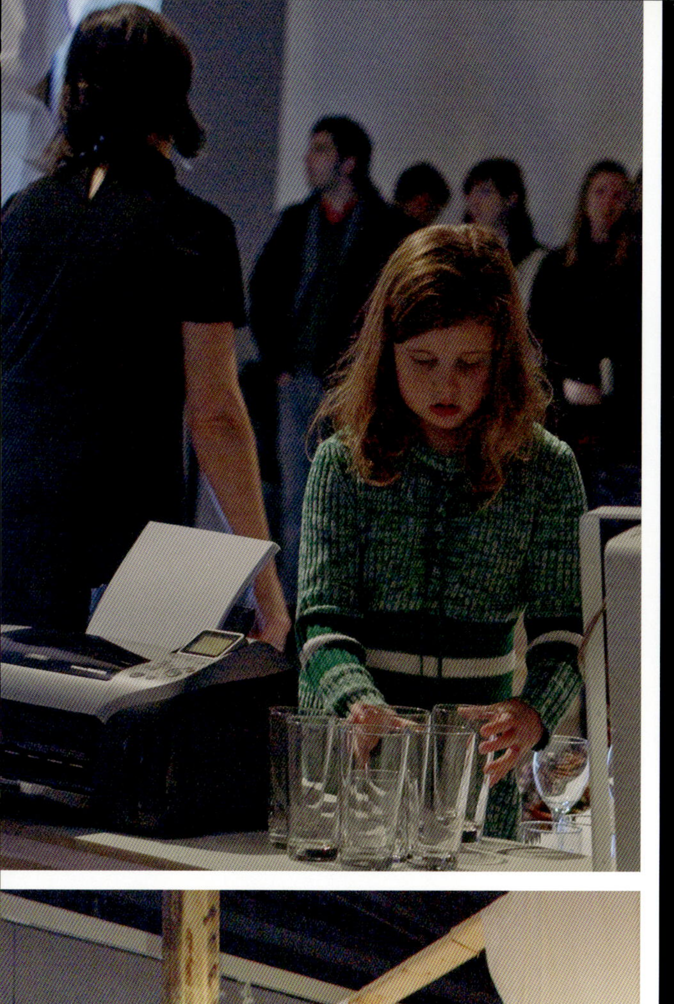
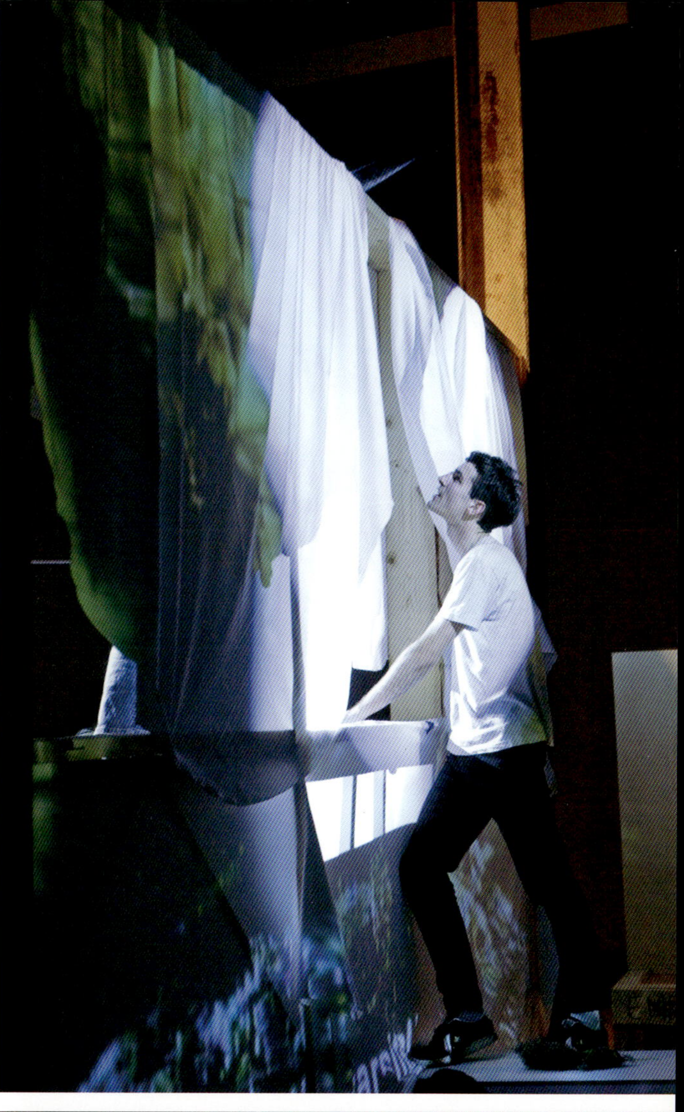
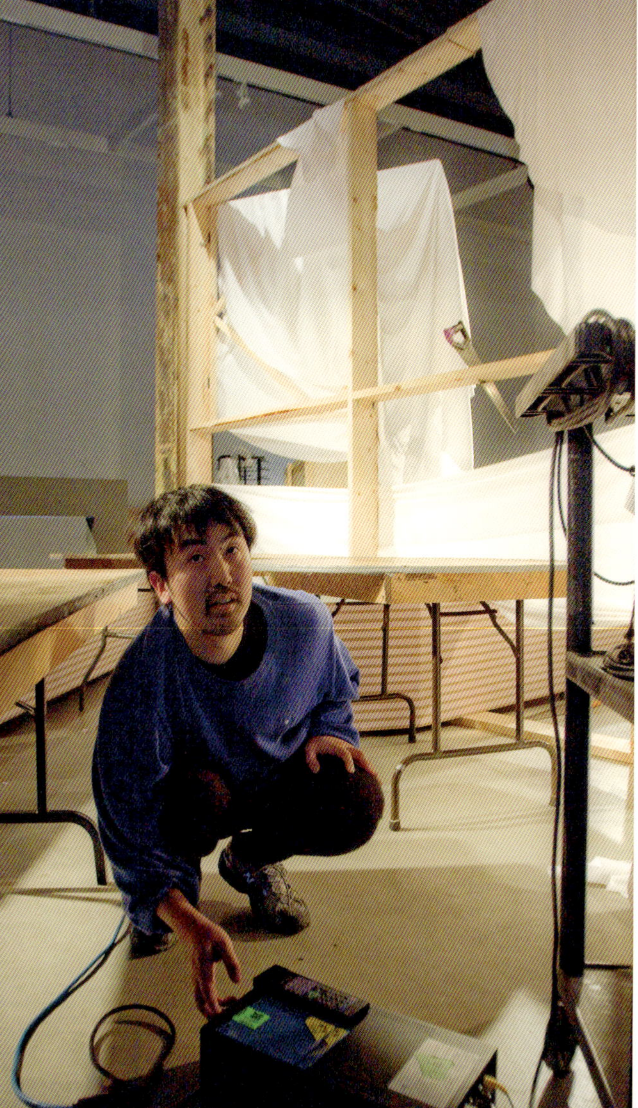
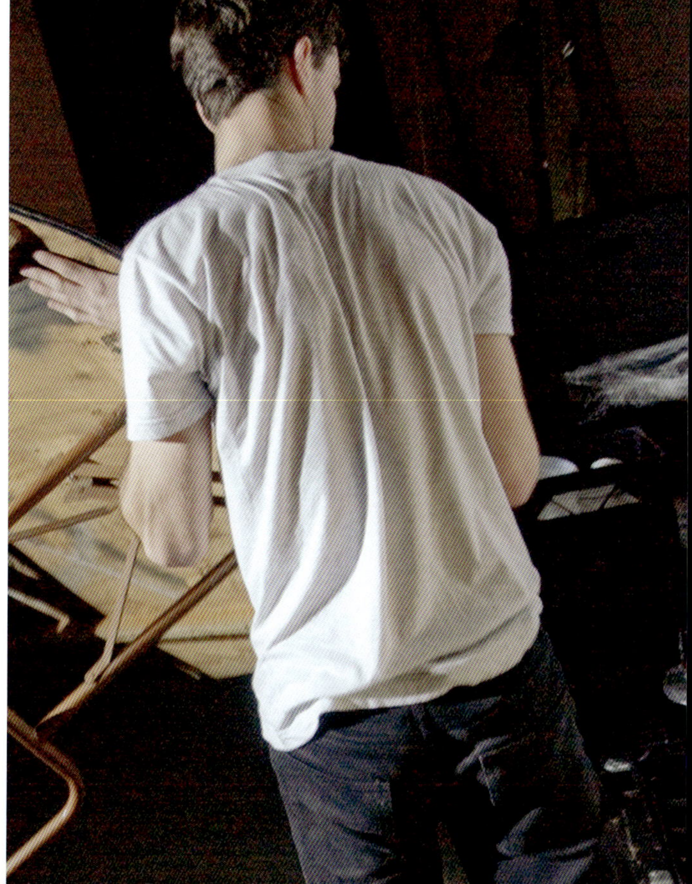

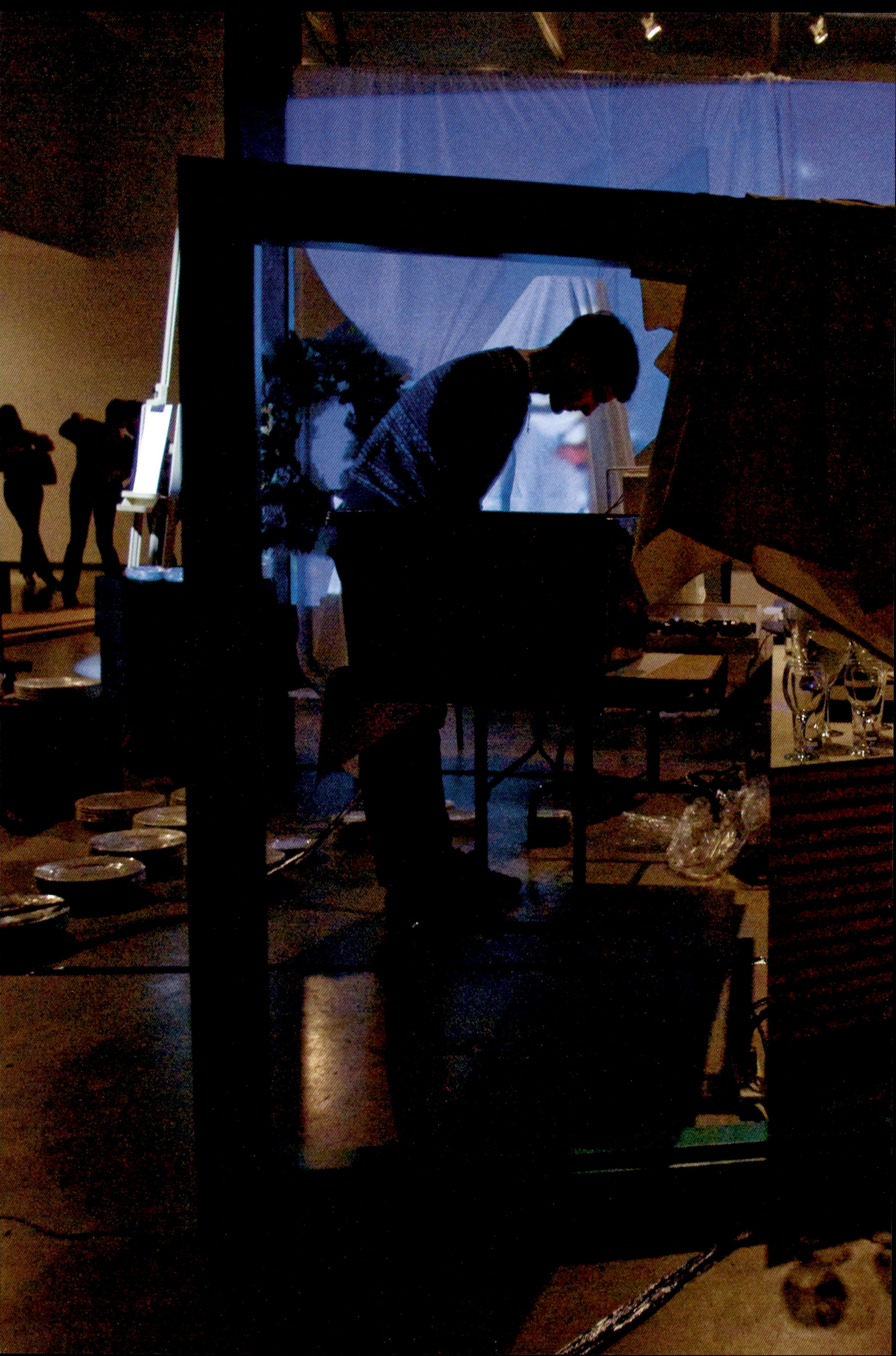

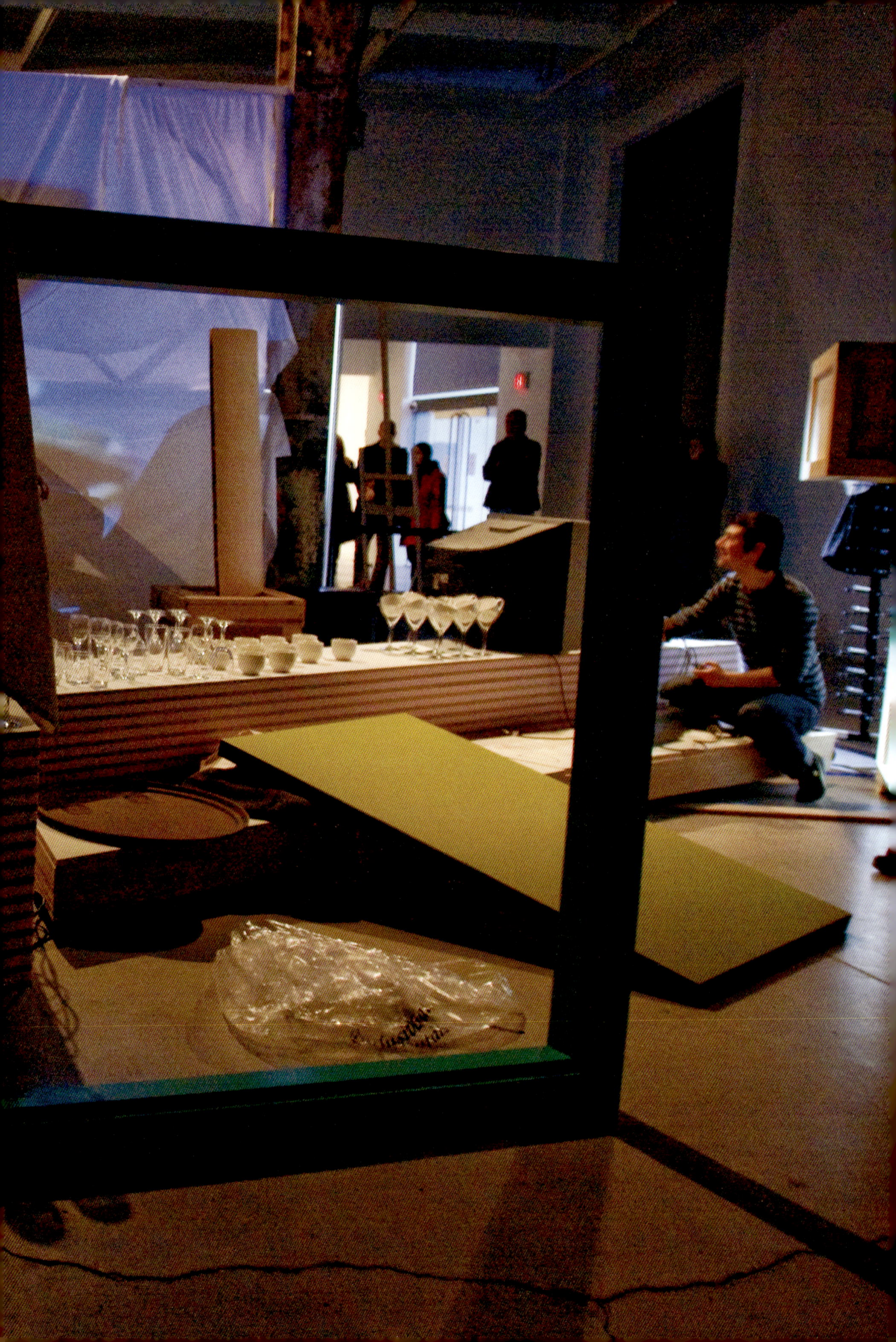

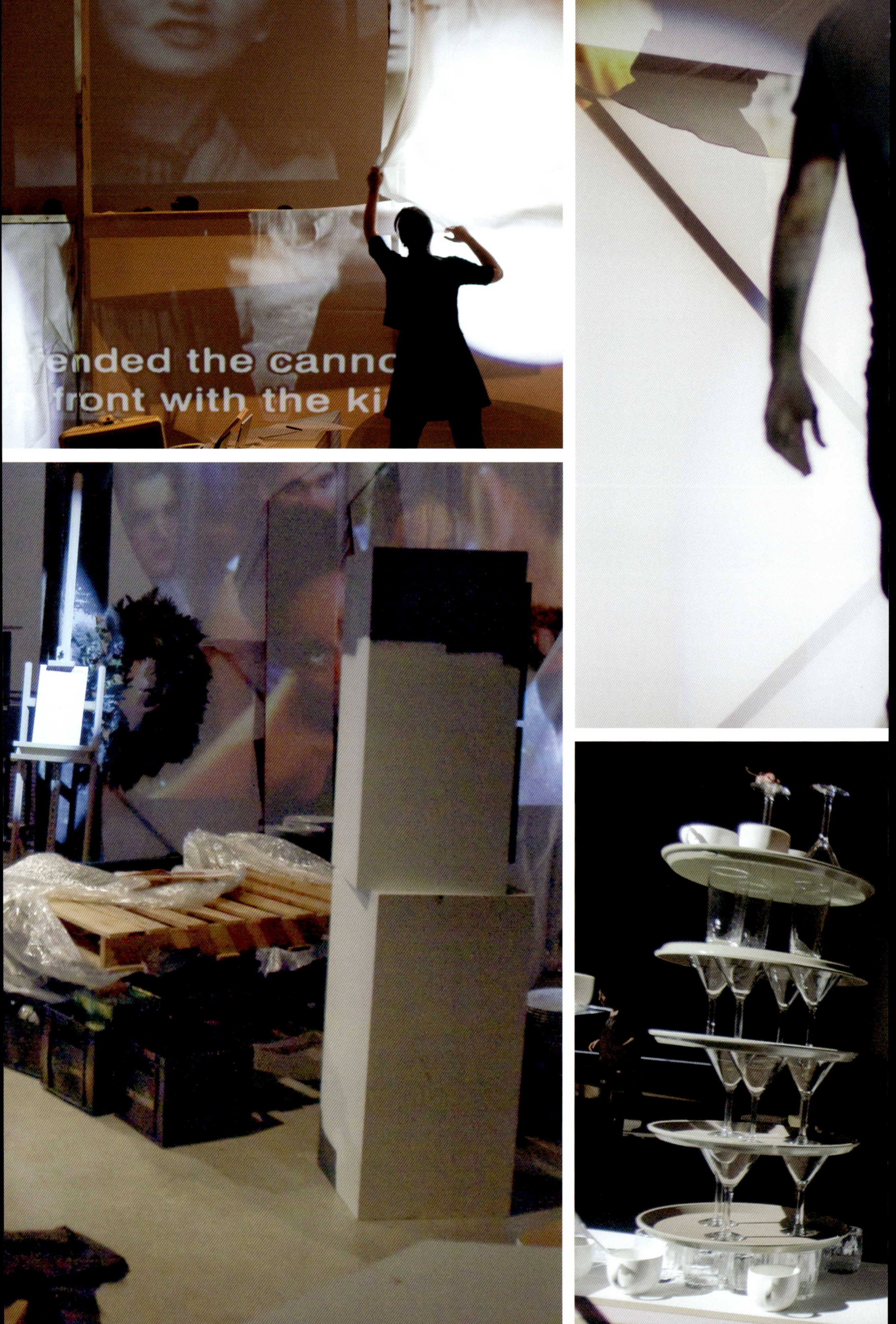
ended the canno
front with the ki

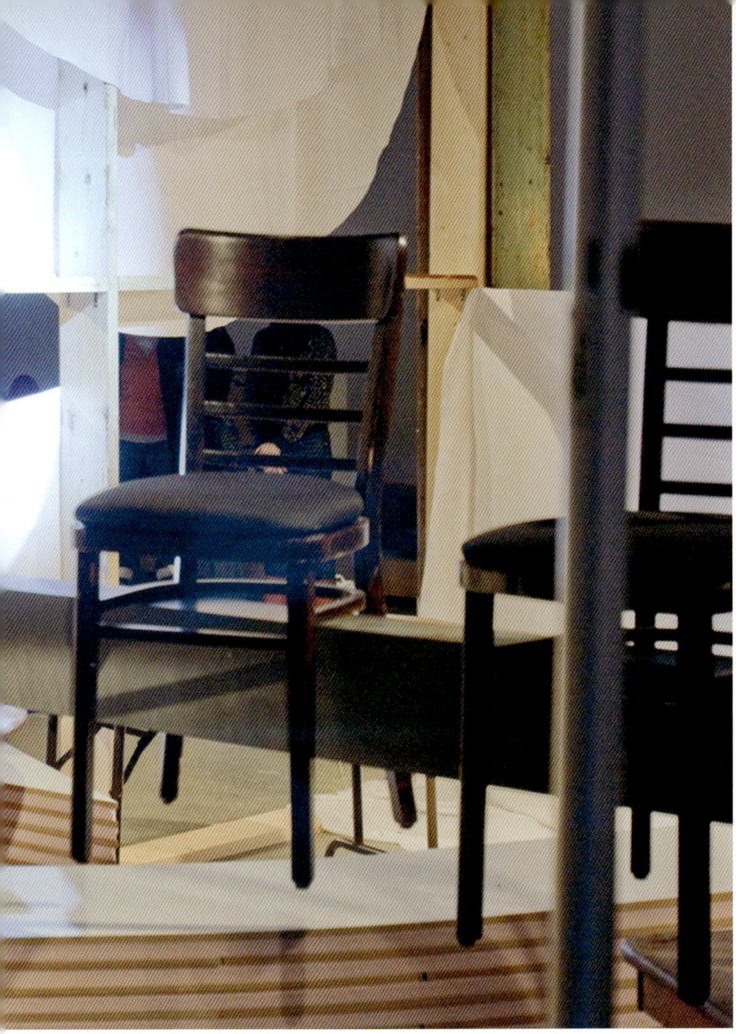

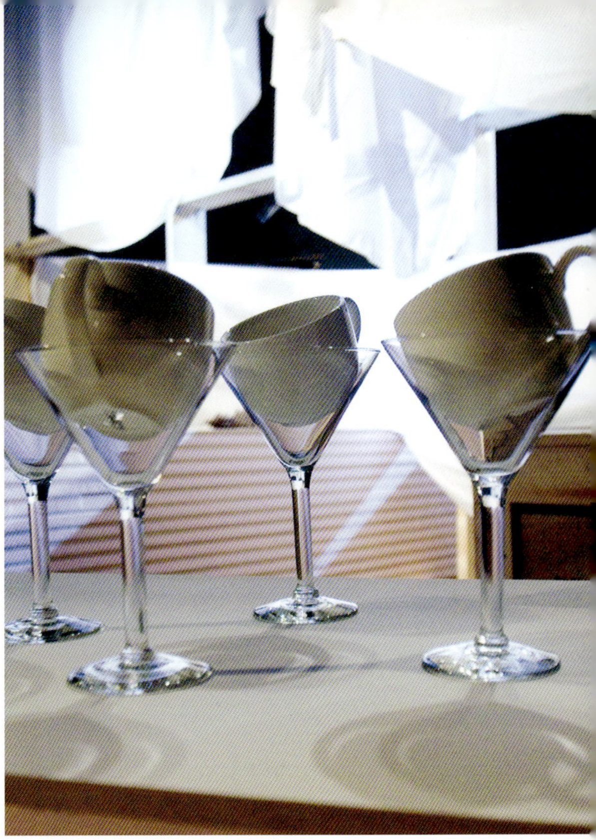

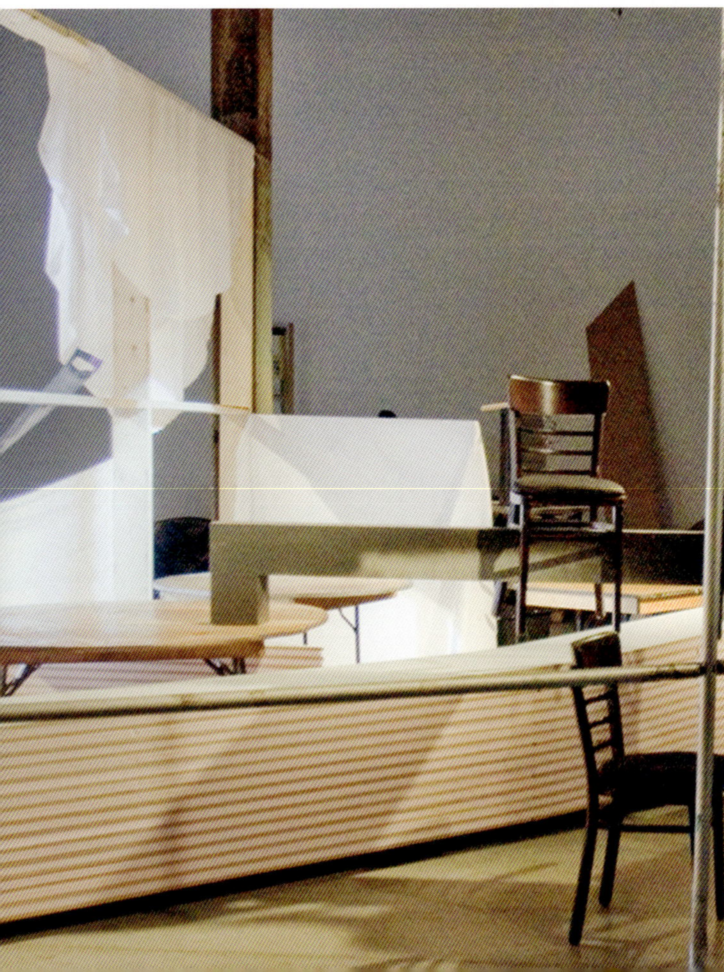
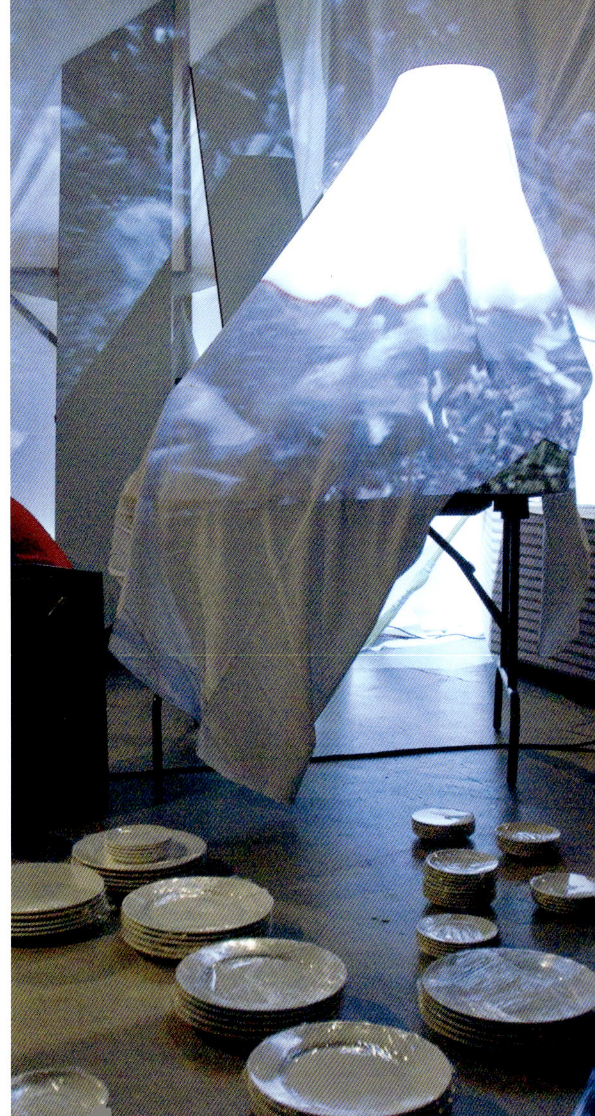

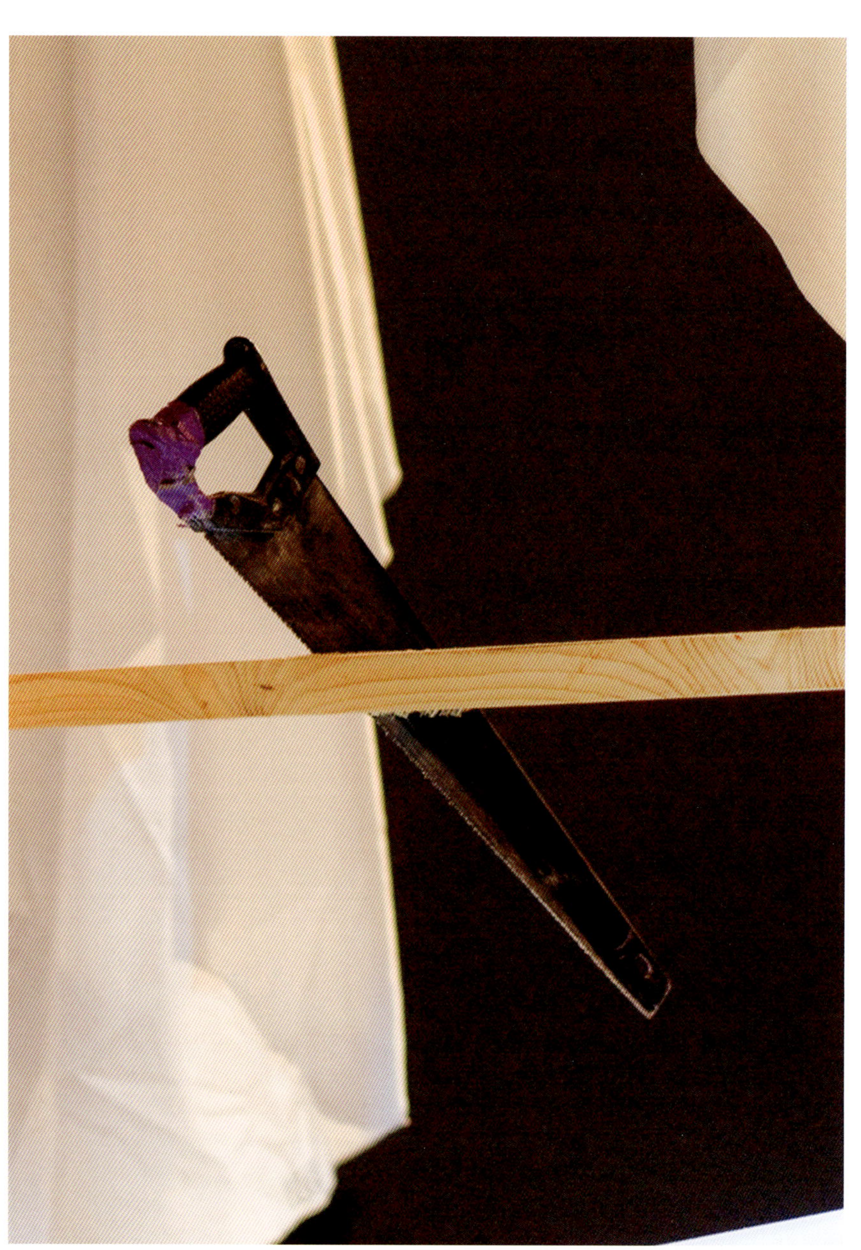

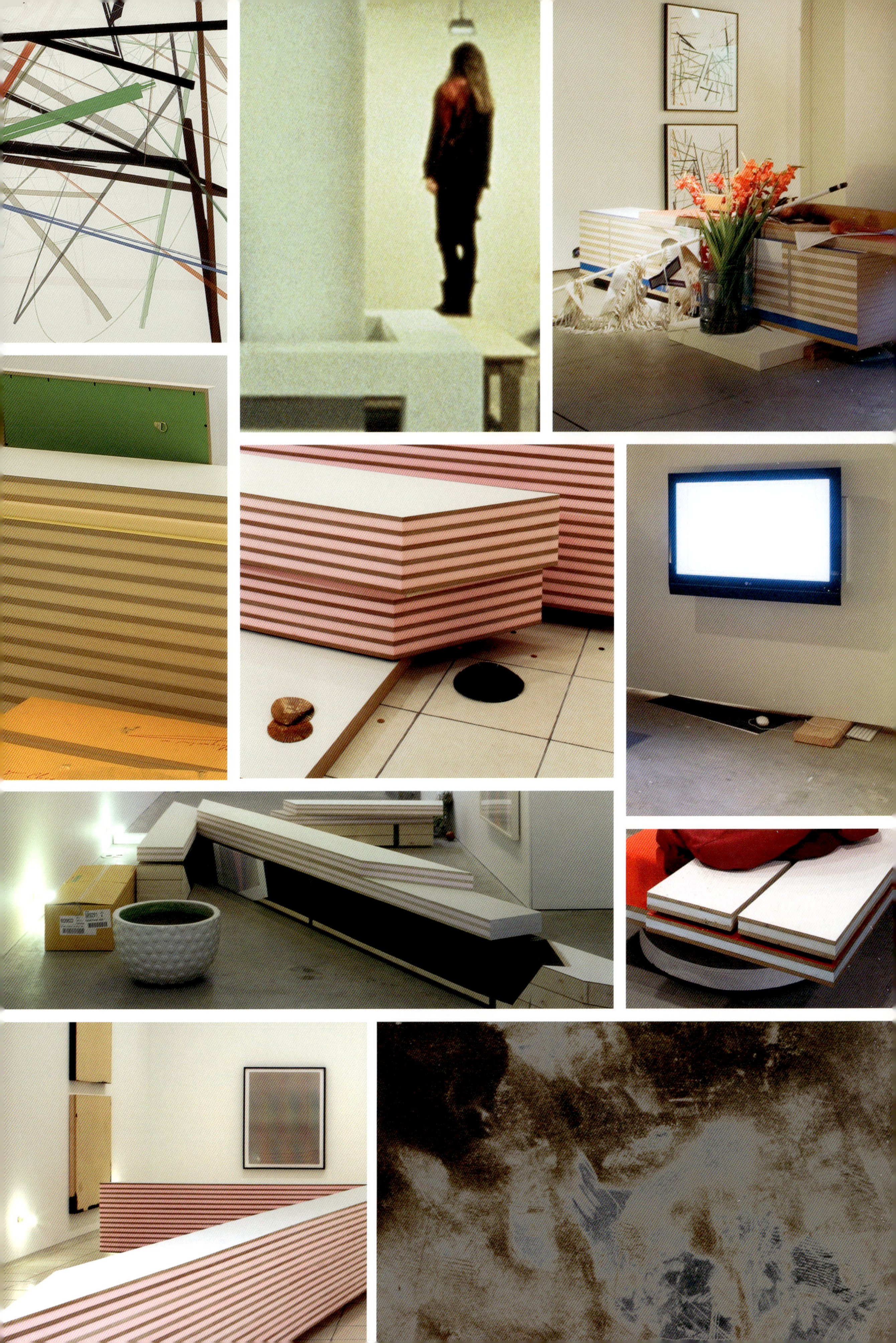

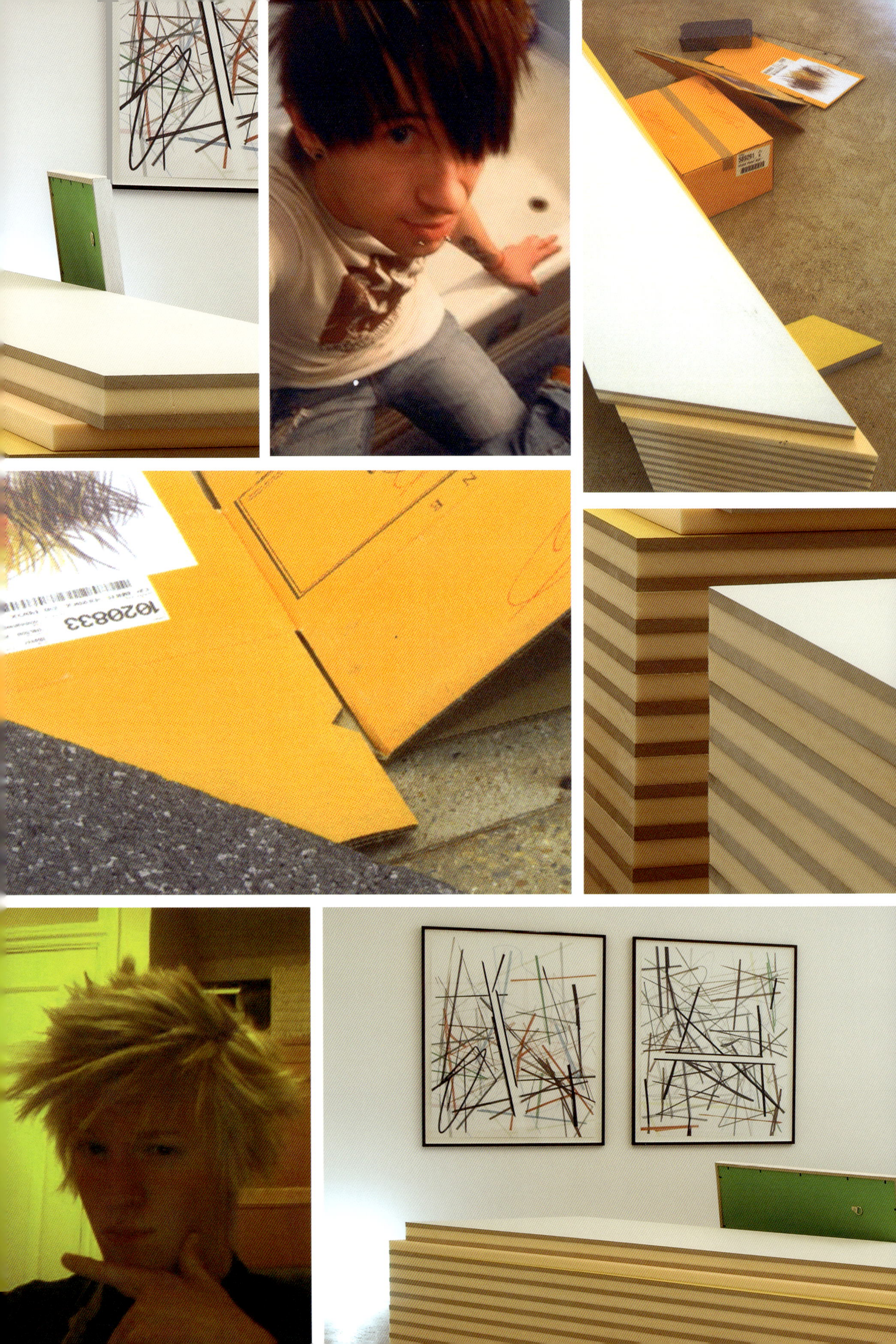

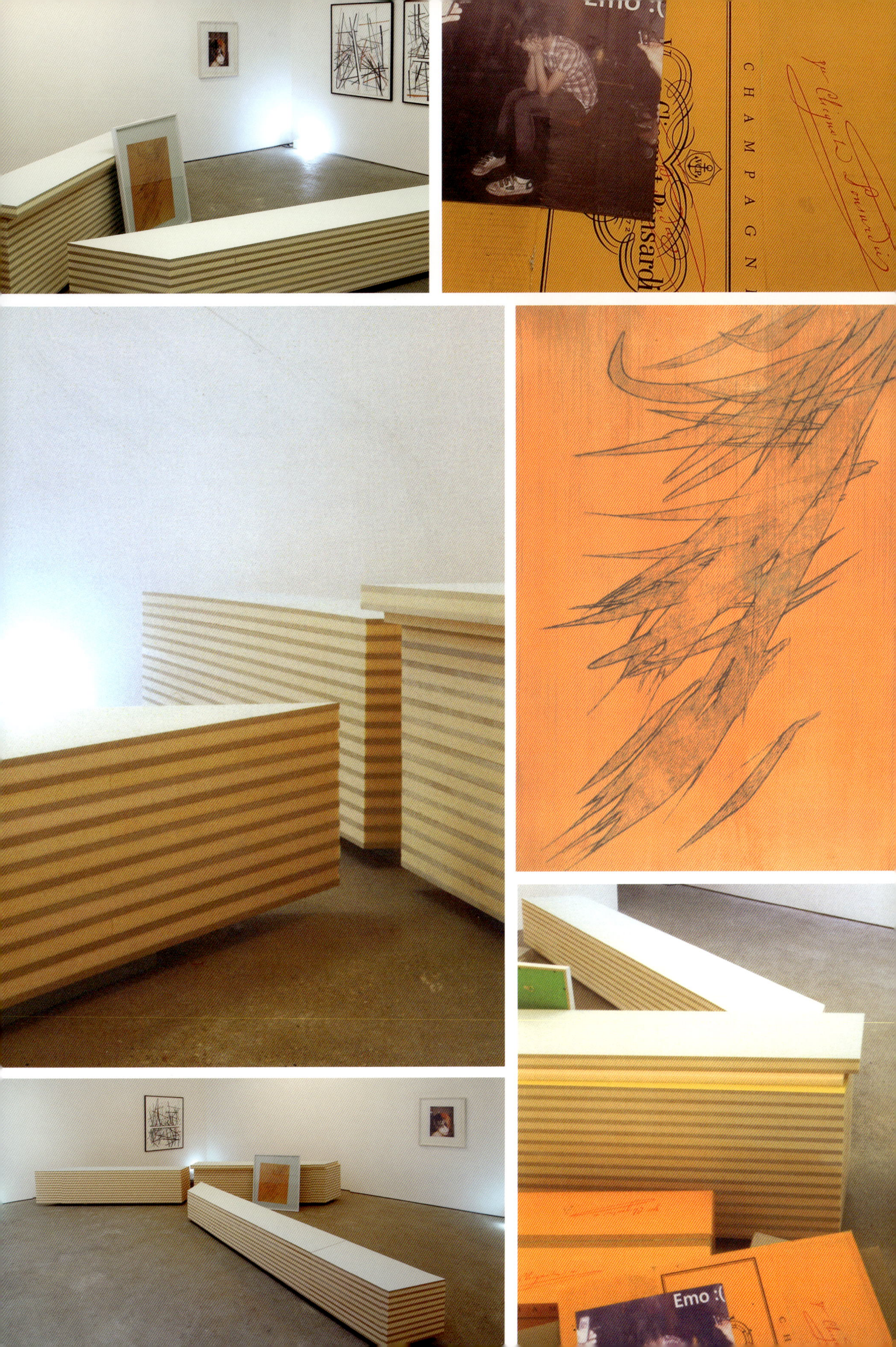

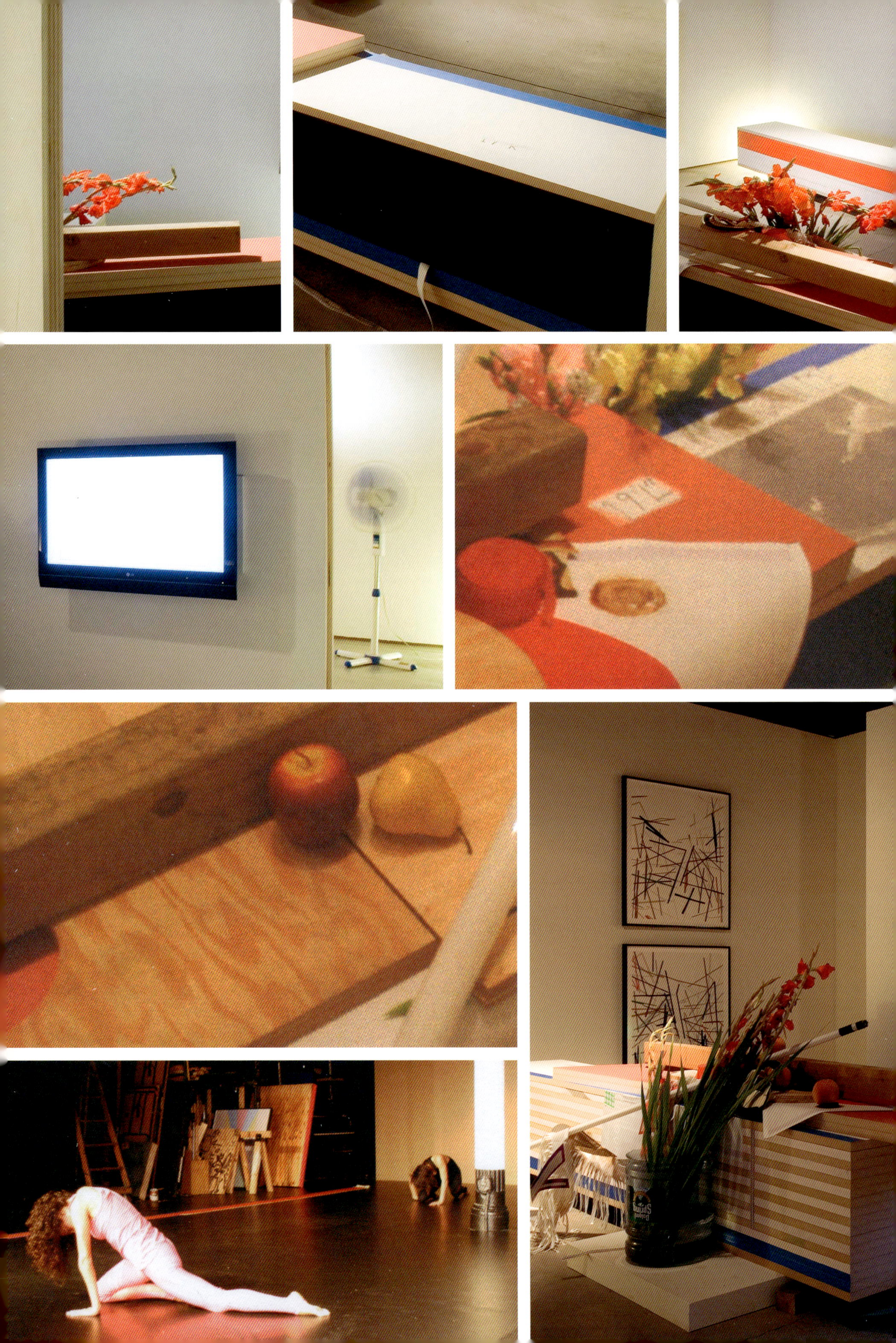

PORTE COUPE-FEU
NE METTEZ PAS D'OBSTACLE
A LA FERMETURE

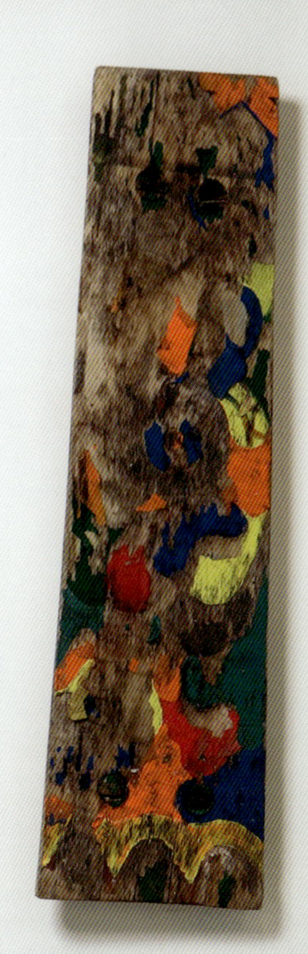

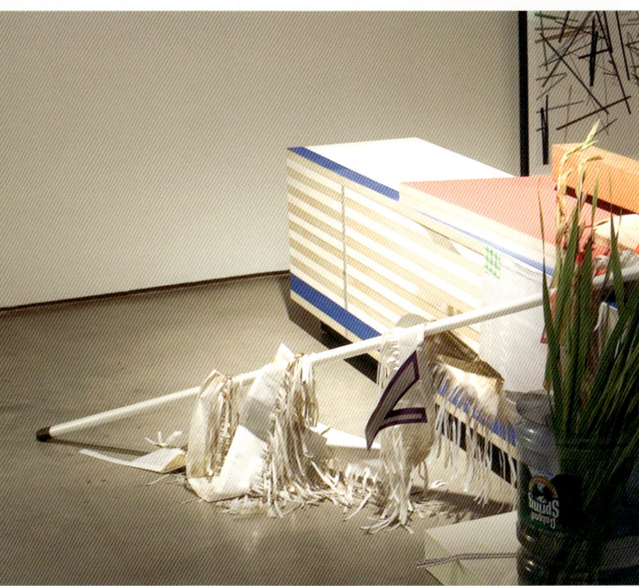

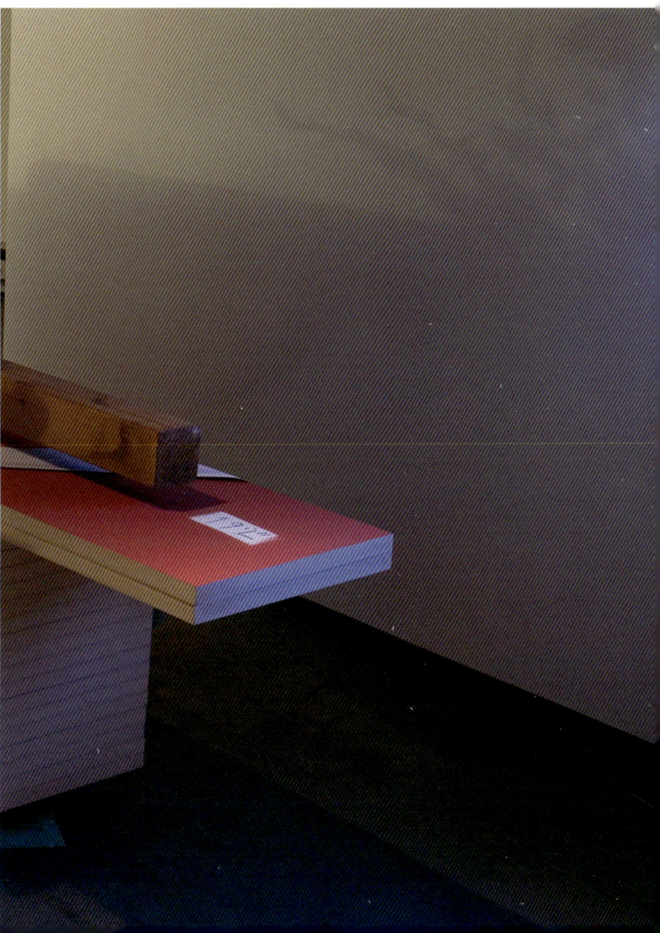

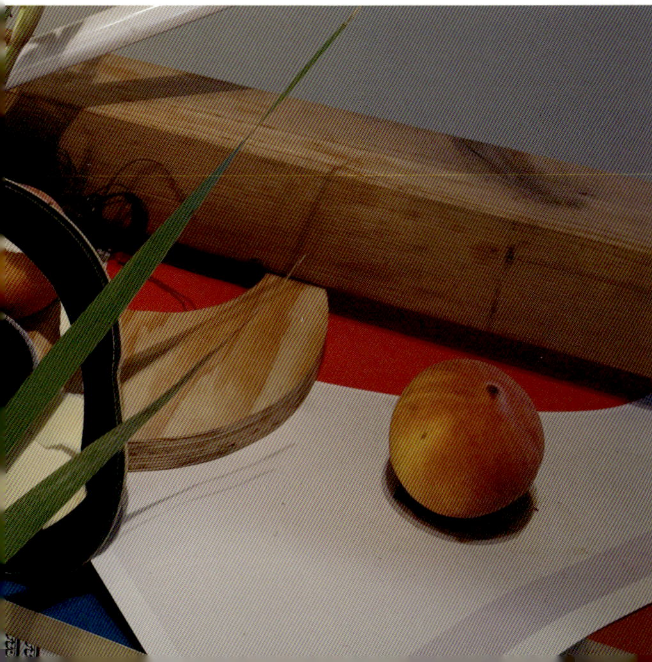

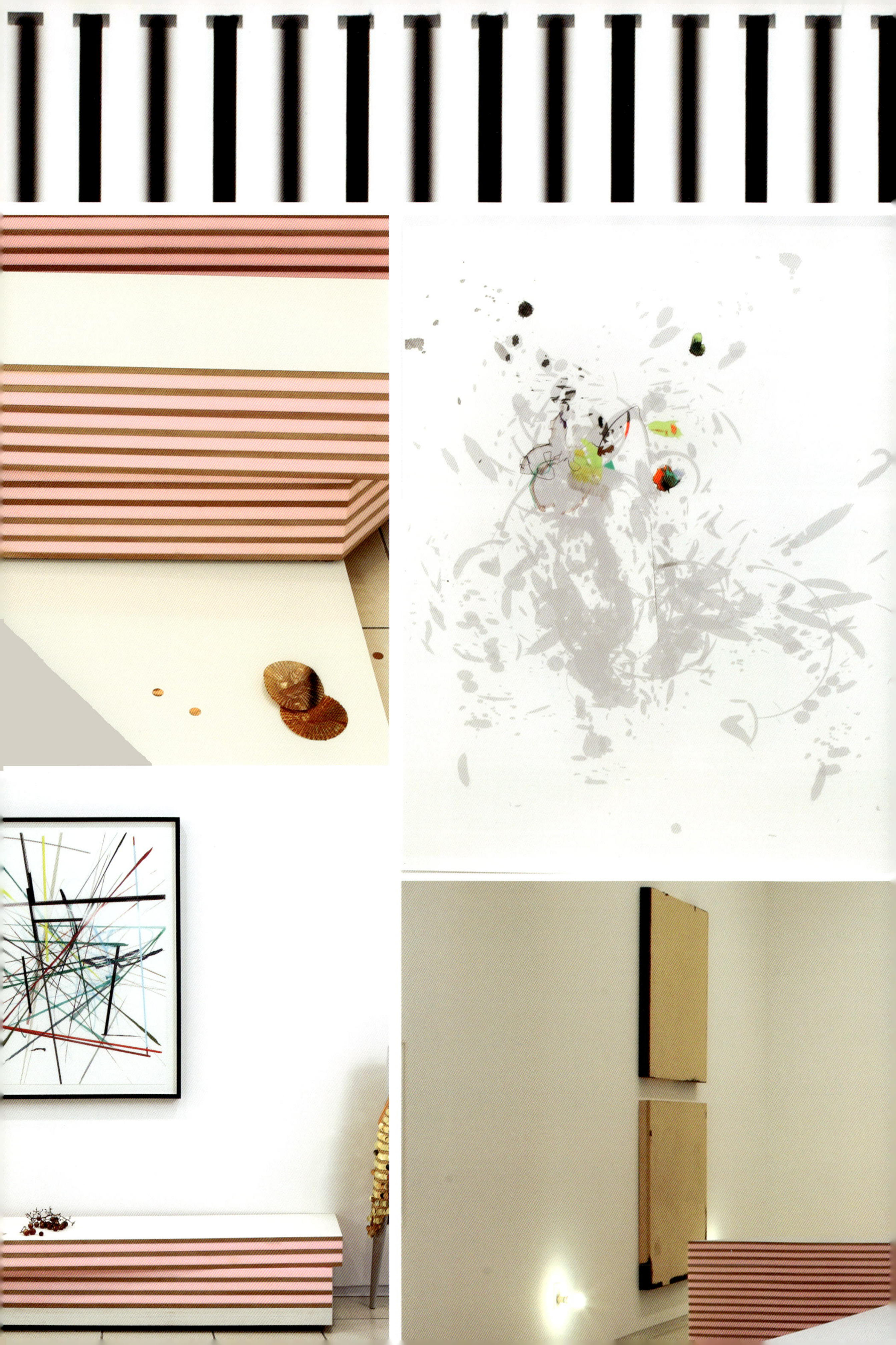

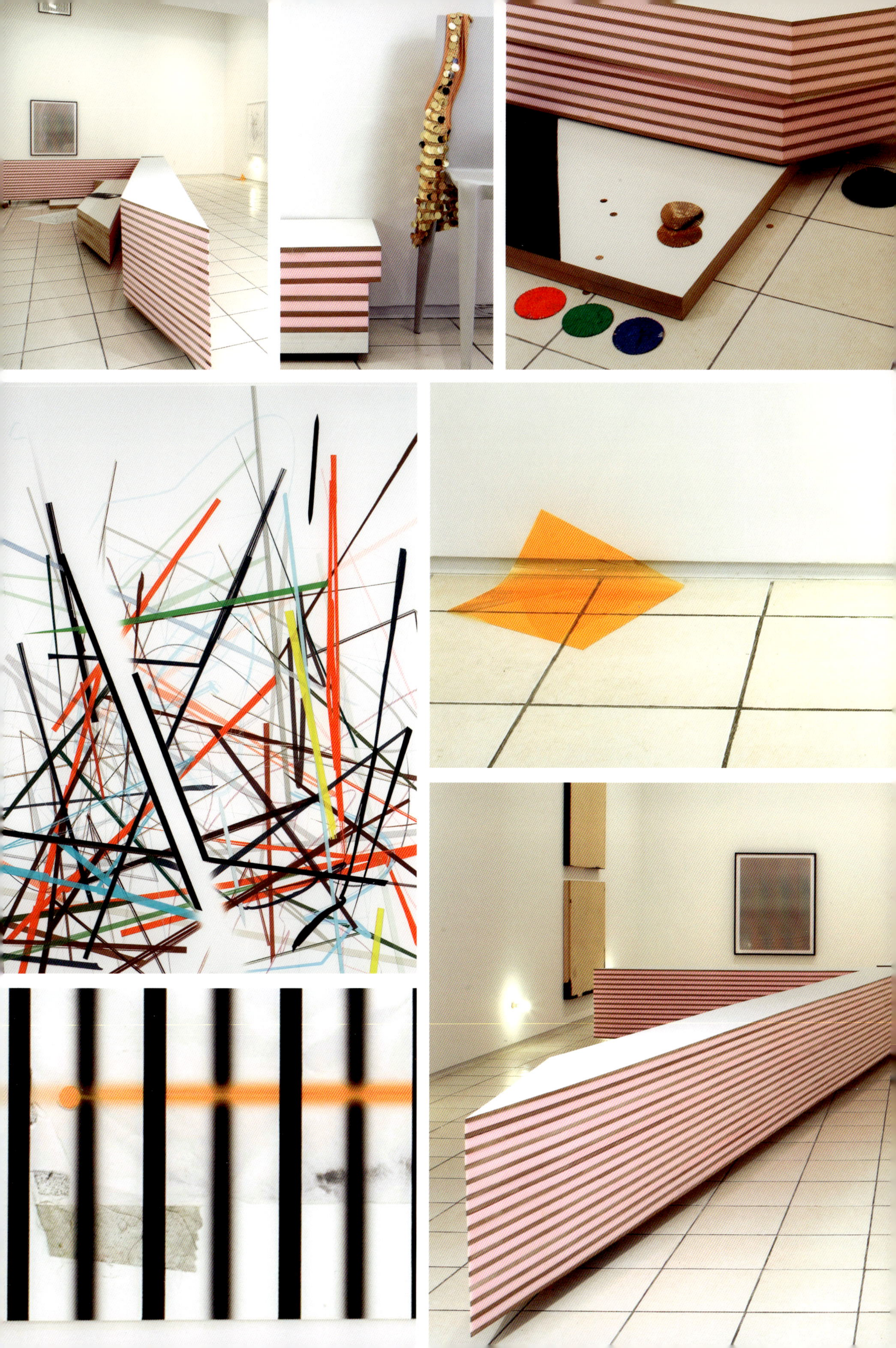

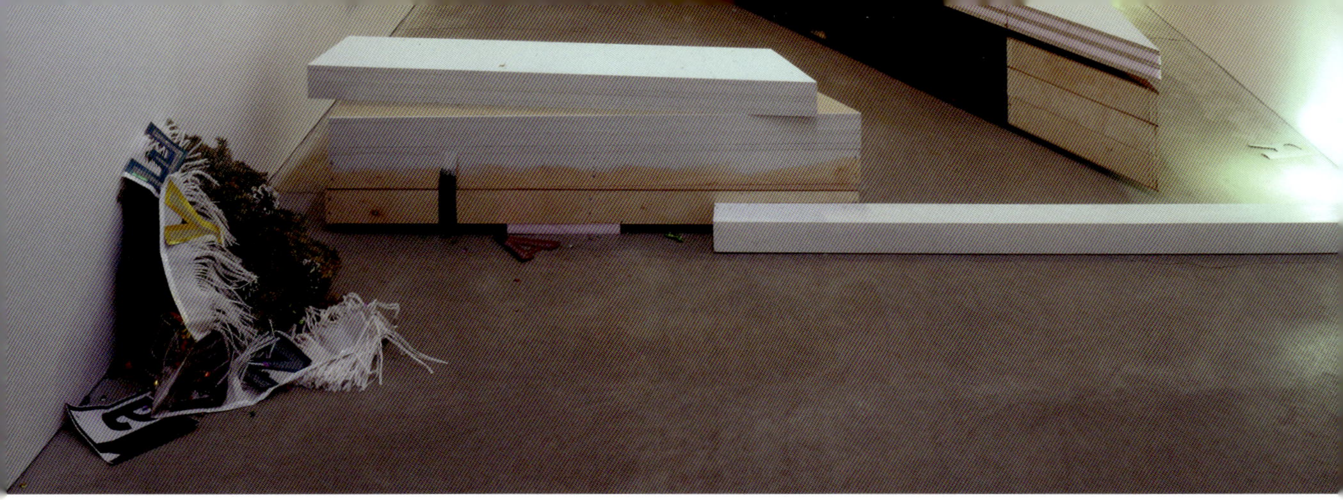

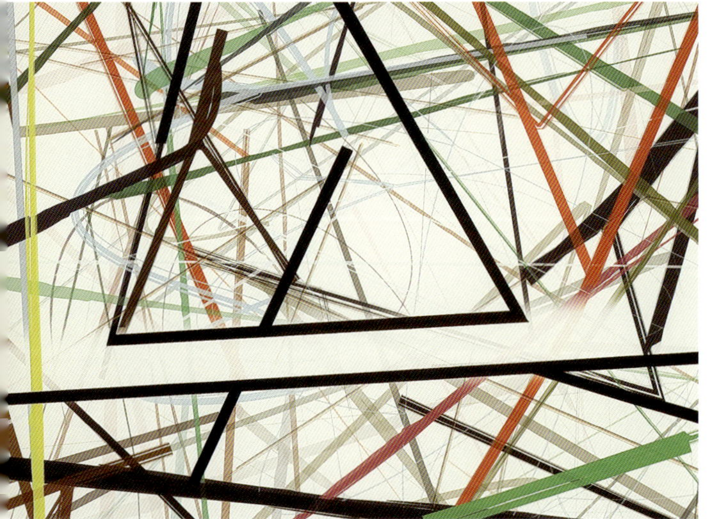

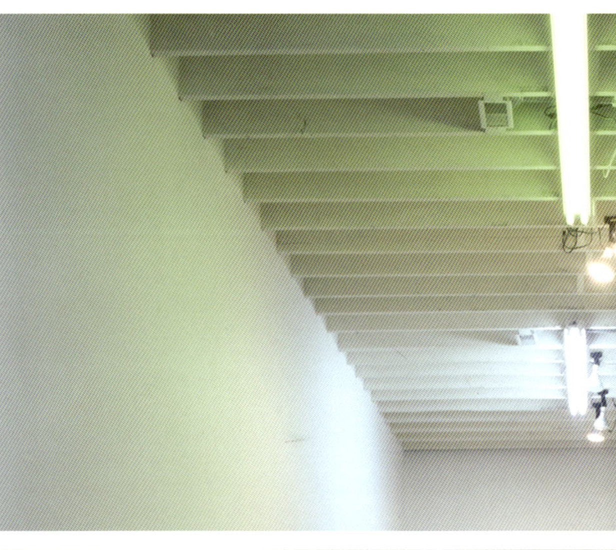

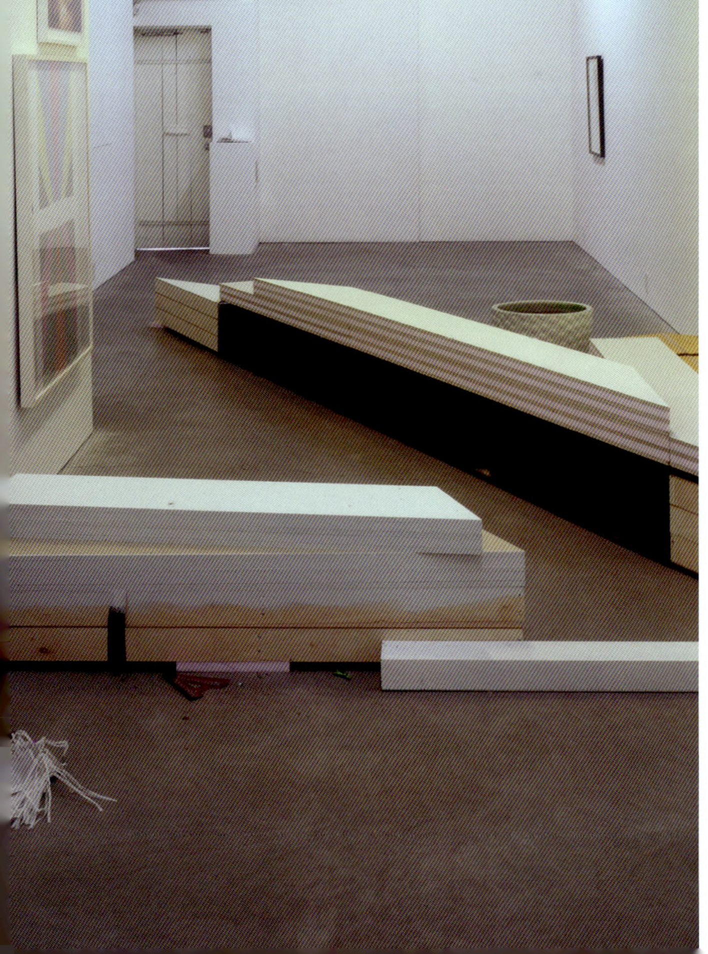

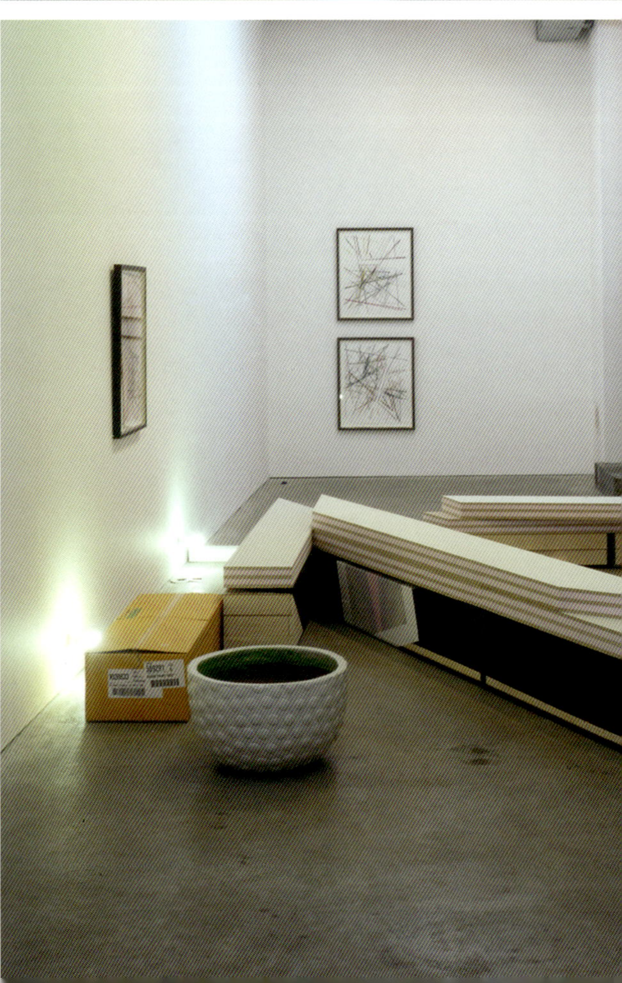

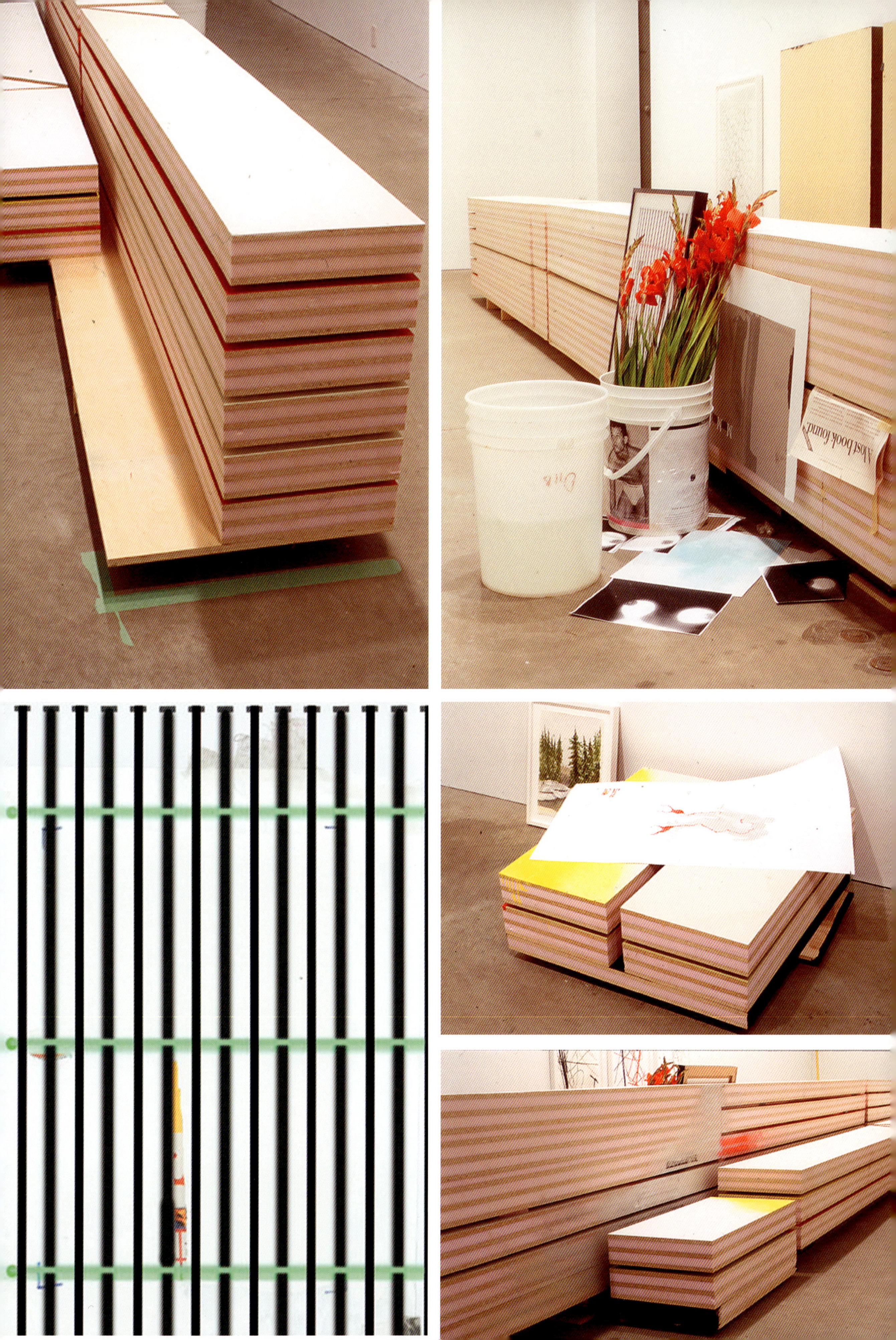

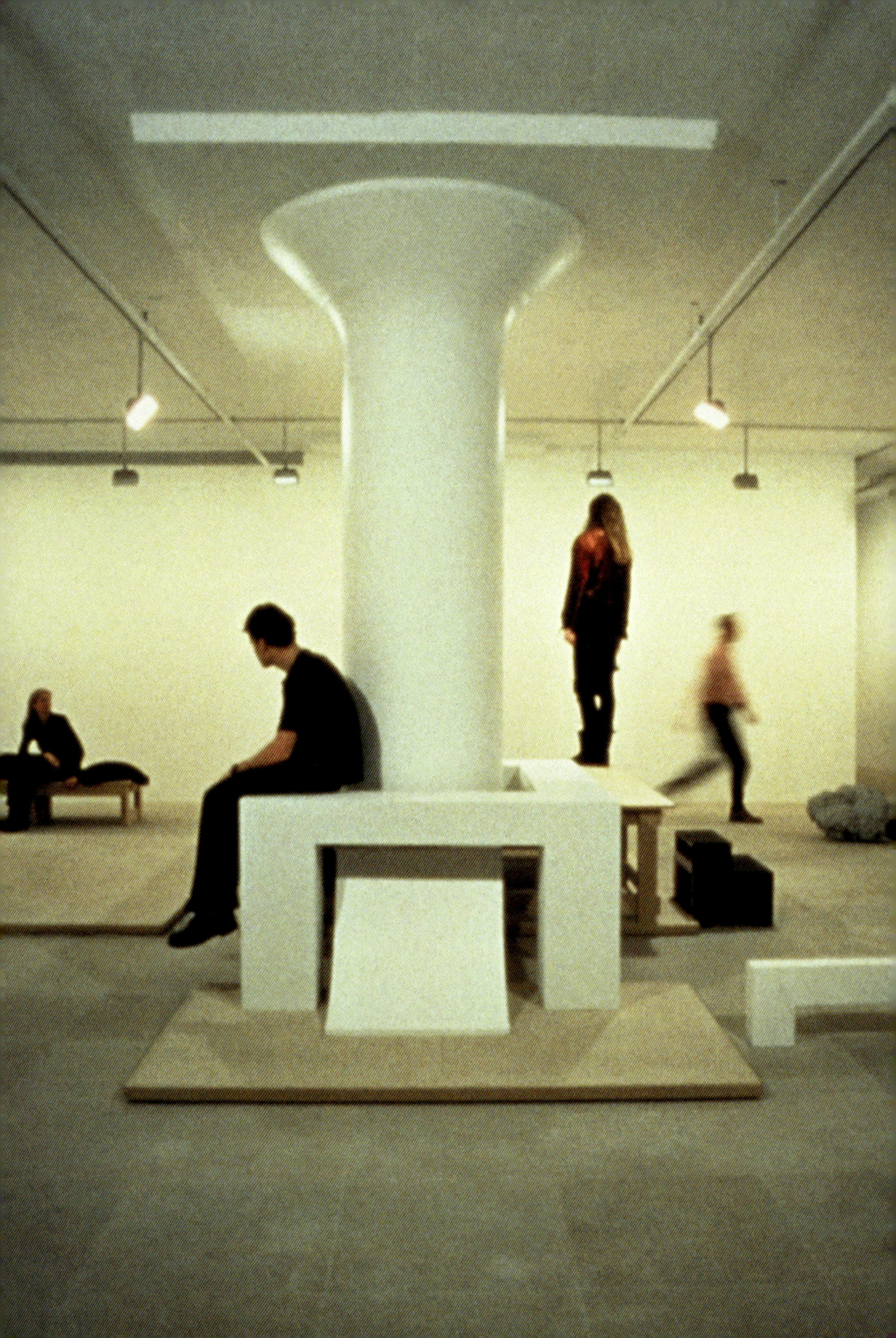

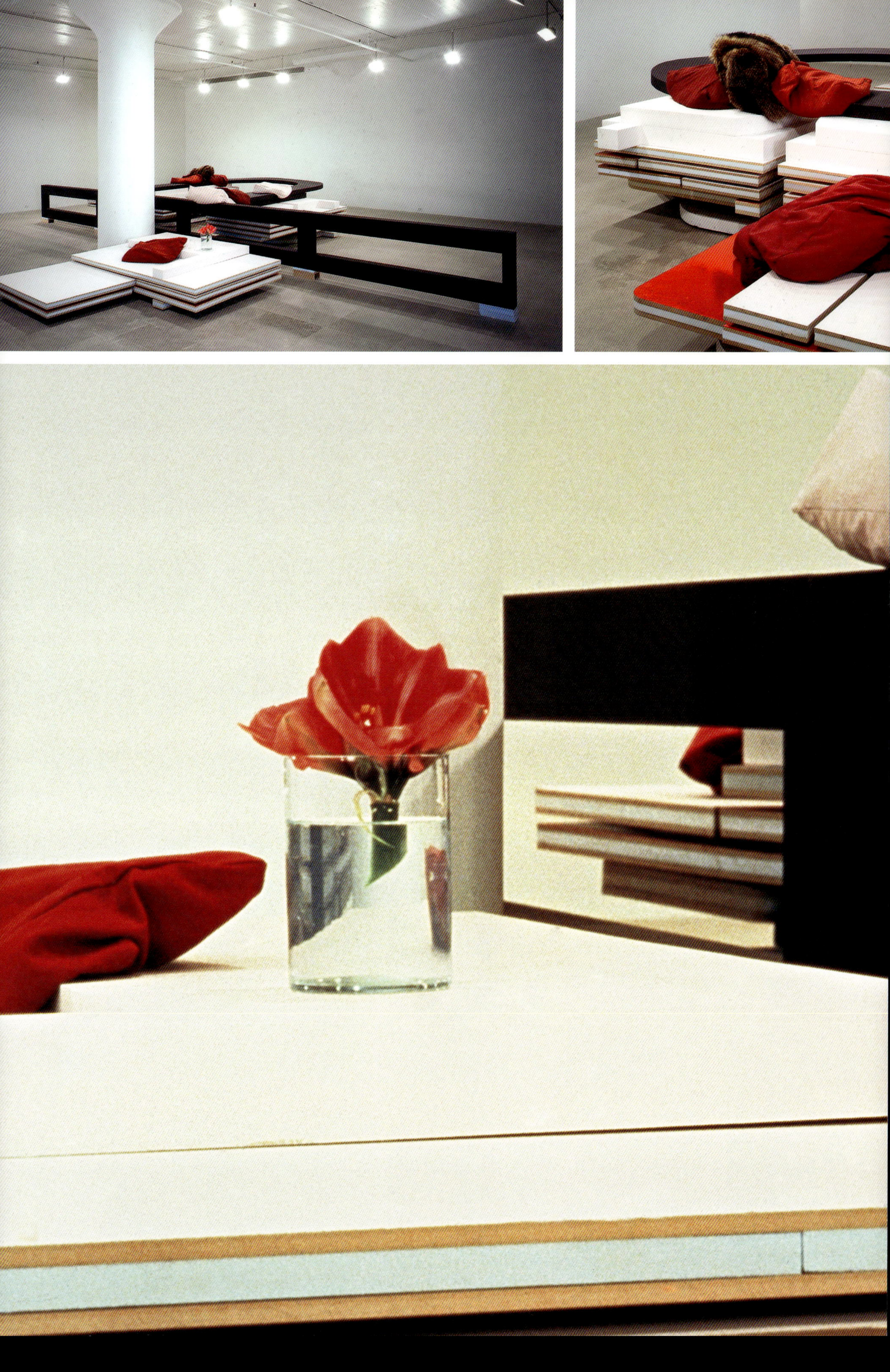

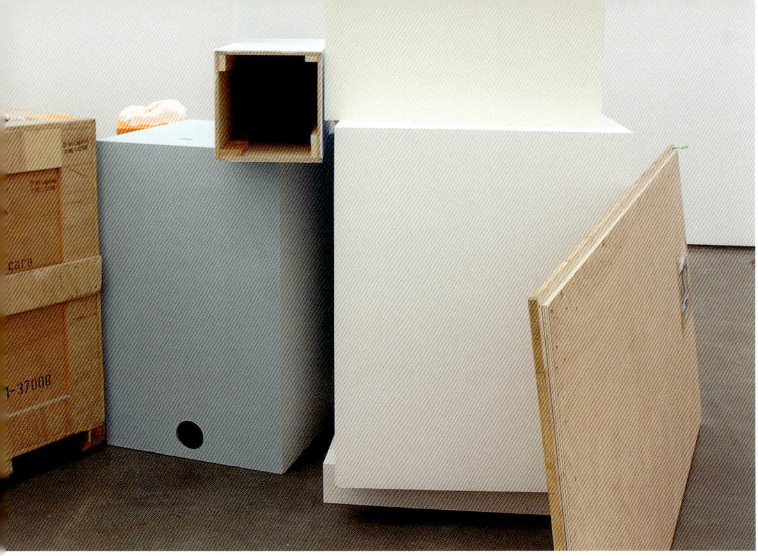

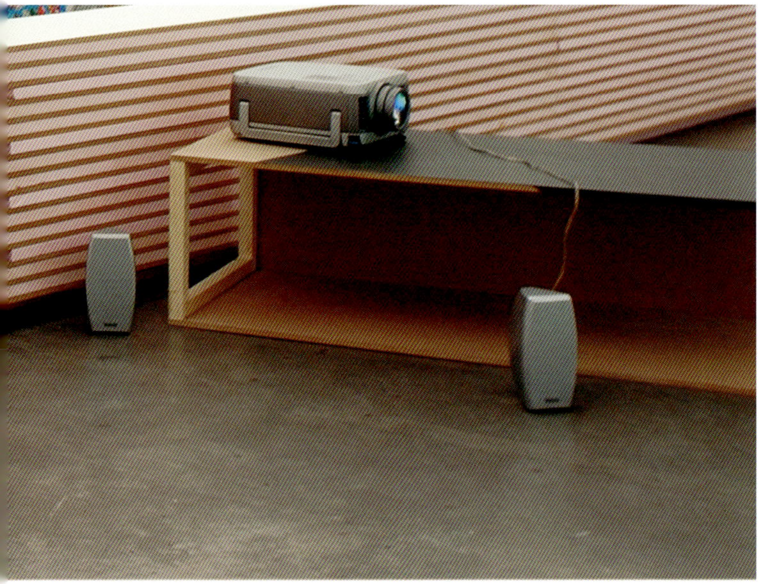

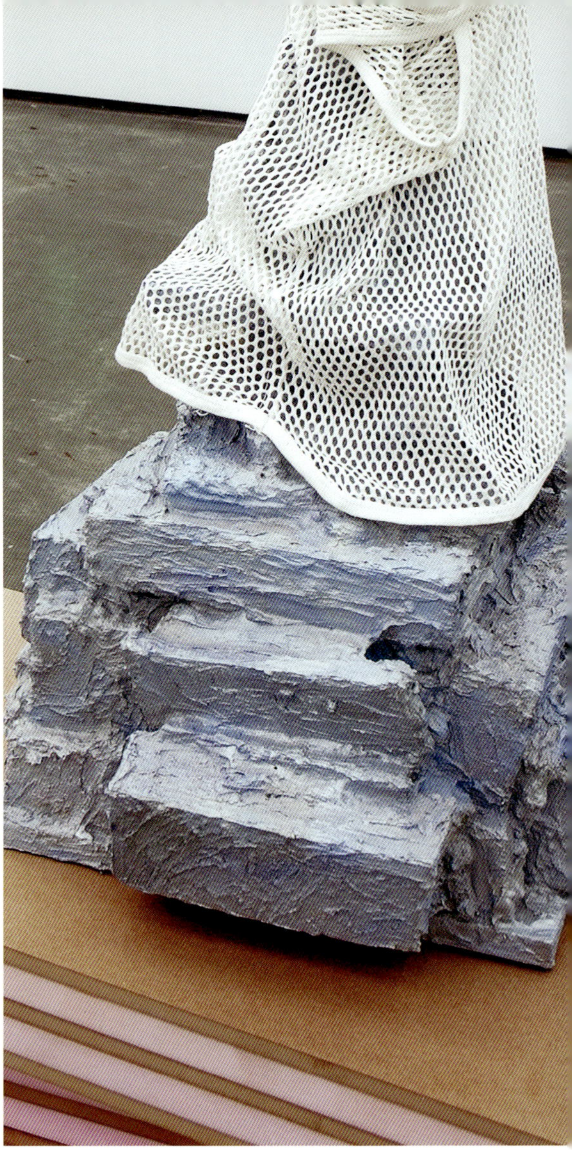

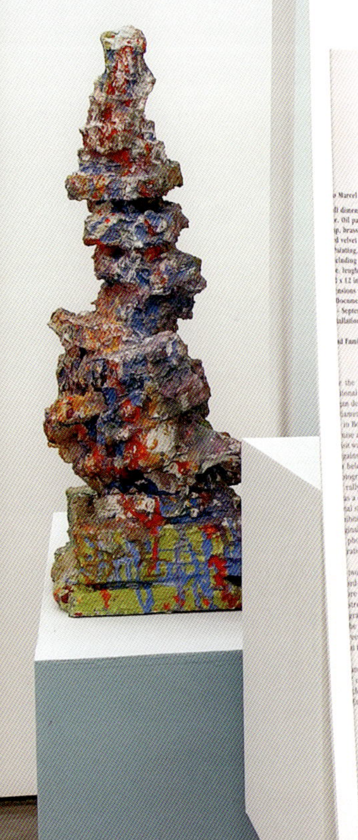

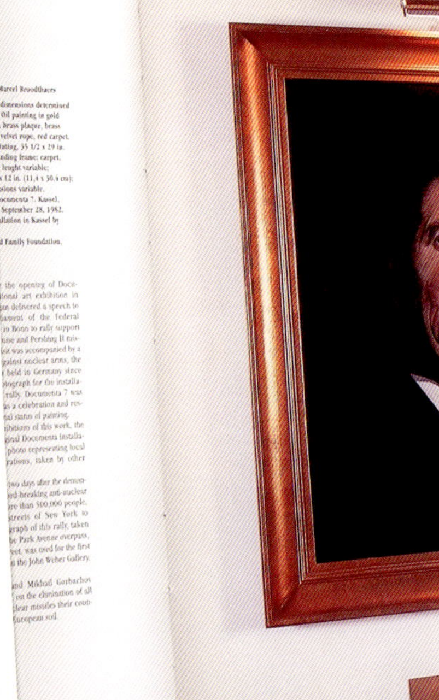

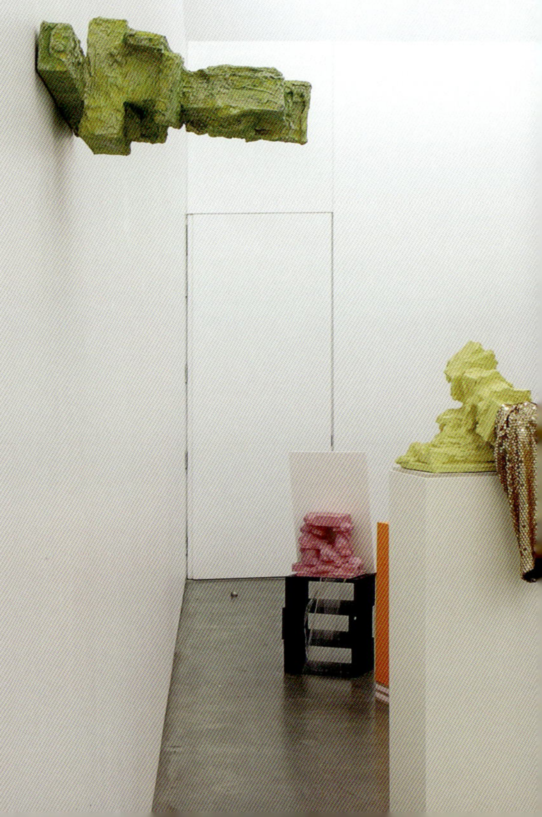

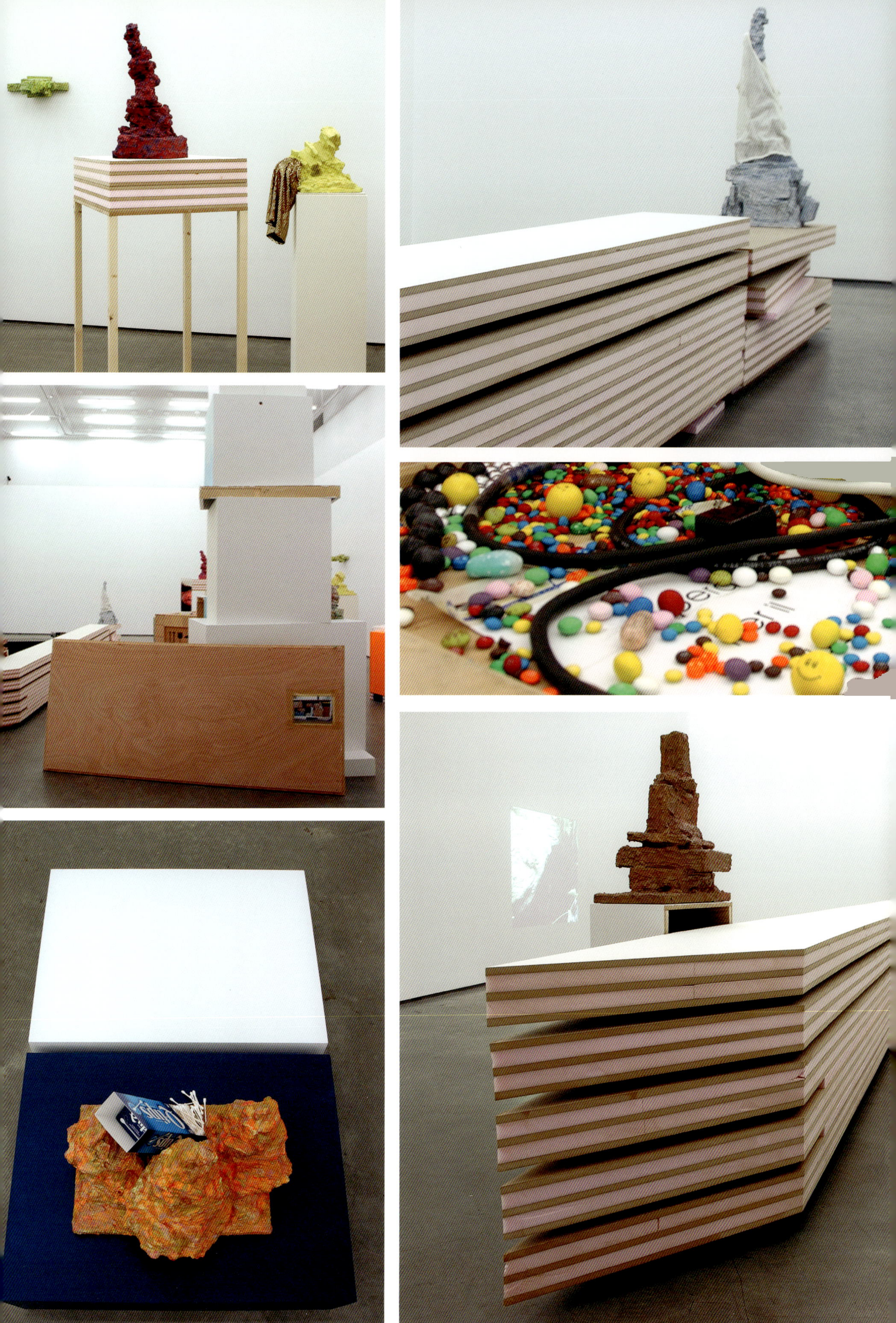

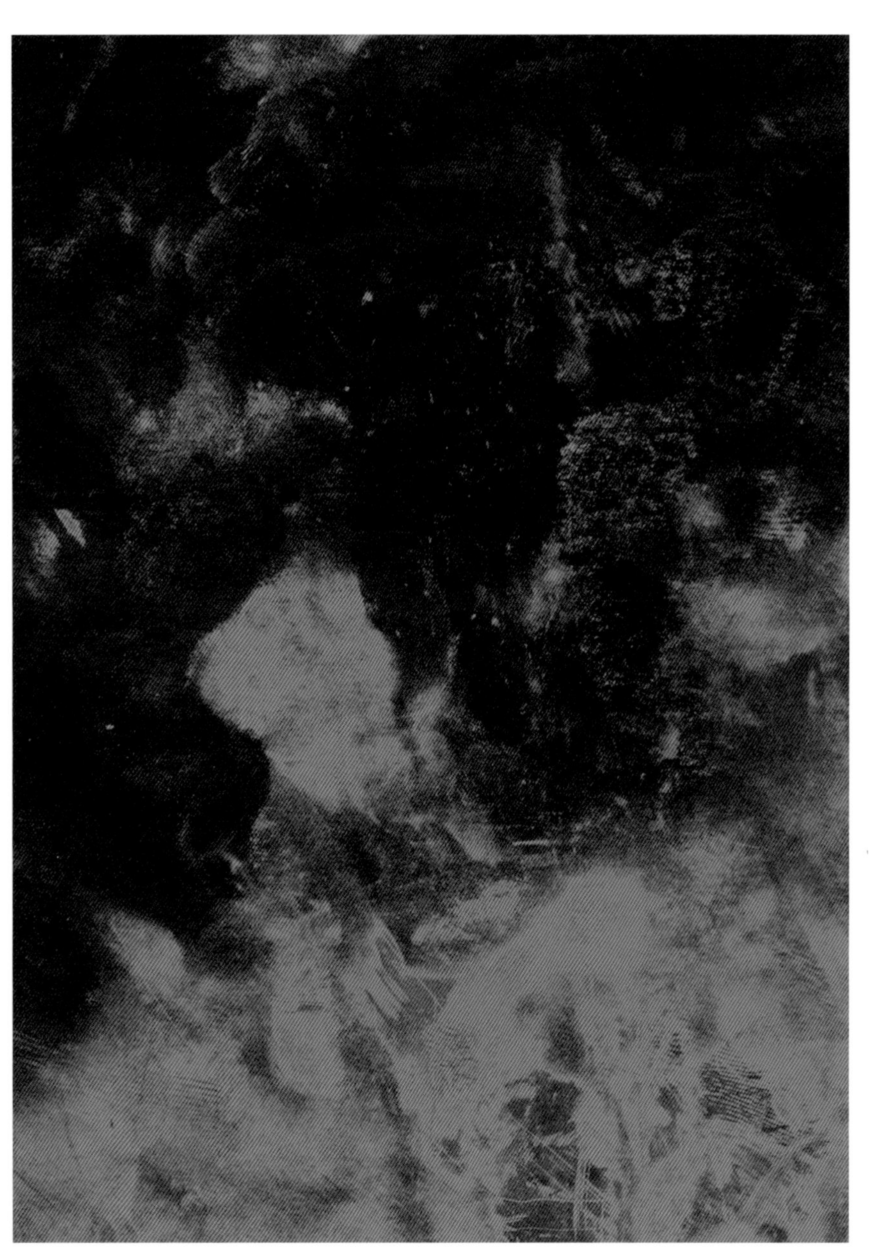

SCOTT LYALL

THE
POWER / LOVER
BALL

ACKNOWLEDGEMENTS

'Scott Lyall: THE POWER BALL' was published to document the exhibition of the same name presented at The Power Plant from 20 September to 23 November 2008. 'Scott Lyall: THE POWER BALL' was the 2008 Commission, realized under The Power Plant's annual Commissioning Program with the support of the 2008–09 Commissioning Partner, Partners in Art (PIA).

The Power Plant is grateful to all members of PIA for supporting the commission and publication. We especially acknowledge the efforts of PIA co-chairs Shabin Mohamed and Eleanor Shen. We extend thanks to RBC, presenting sponsor of the exhibition 'Scott Lyall: THE POWER BALL.' Thanks also go to Exhibition Support Sponsor Westbury National Show Systems Ltd., and Exhibition Support Donor Miguel Abreu Gallery, New York. Further thanks to Exclusive Affairs Rentals, for their support of the exhibition, and Susan Hobbs Gallery, Toronto. General thanks go to Dawn Brammer, Dee Gibson of Catering with Style, Michael Haddad, Rachel Harrison, Maria Hassabi, Susan Hobbs, Blake Rayne and Carol Weinbaum.

We also gratefully acknowledge PIA Artrageous co-chairs Tamara Bahry Paterson and Jennifer Tanenbaum.

Finally, we are indebted to Scott Lyall for realizing the exceptional exhibition and commission, THE POWER BALL.

2008–09 COMMISSIONING PARTNER

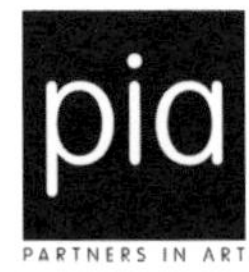

EXHIBITION PRESENTING SPONSOR

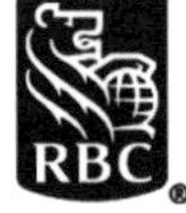

EXHIBITION SUPPORT SPONSORS

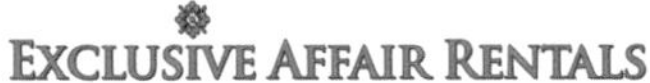

EXHIBITION AND PUBLICATION SUPPORT SPONSOR

MIGUEL ABREU GALLERY

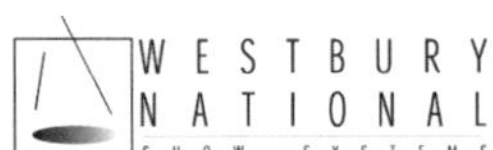

CATALOGUE SUPPORT

Susan Hobbs

CONTENTS

INTRODUCTION: THE ⟨POWER⟩ BALL

Gregory Burke

In the months leading up to the opening of THE ⟨POWER⟩ BALL by Scott Lyall at The Power Plant, Lyall also worked on his installation for SITE Santa Fe's Seventh International Biennial, which opened in June 2008. While not formally linked, the launches of these installations bookended the northern summer, which started with art and commodities markets at record levels and concluded with the credit crunch and the ensuing crisis in the world banking system. In retrospect these installations can in some senses be seen to be prophetic of this shift. The Santa Fe installation involved local painters working with Lyall to produce a mural, recalling the Depression-era murals realized in New Mexico under the New Deal initiative. Adjacent to the mural Lyall positioned a small abstract composition, itself an appropriation of the RE/MAX Realty logo that sports the colours of the United States flag underneath a hot air balloon. Lyall's reference to real estate coincided with the mounting rumblings of the sub-prime mortgage saga. By September the balloon had burst and many viewers read Lyall's THE ⟨POWER⟩ BALL as a particularly poignant metaphor for a dramatic change in economic conditions. While Lyall may not be averse to such readings, he would assert that they highlight the viewer's active role in defining the context for interpretation of his work. In reading THE ⟨POWER⟩ BALL as emblematic, the viewer ascribes the installation the quality of image; a dramatized scene they can walk into and affect and be affected by. In this sense, with THE ⟨POWER⟩ BALL the viewer was engaged performatively by Lyall as a conduit for a consideration of art's connection to the relationship between matter, material and materialism.

THE ⟨POWER⟩ BALL both continues and reprises an interest in aspects of performance evident in Lyall's work over the last decade. As his largest exhibition to date, THE ⟨POWER⟩ BALL falls somewhere between a survey of Lyall's past work and an entirely new assemblage. It was also The Power Plant's 2008 Commission, realized under the gallery's annual Commissioning Program. In working with contemporary artists to present surveys of their practice, The Power Plant frequently invites the artist to be engaged fully in the curatorial process, as opposed to the gallery adopting the more standard curatorial role of selecting discreet works from an artist's oeuvre. The result can confound the traditional notion of the "retrospective," by including works made over an extended period under the guise of an entirely new project. This was the case with THE ⟨POWER⟩ BALL where Lyall drew from seven previous projects involving performance. These projects include two solo shows at Greene Naftali, New York (1996/1998); the photographic project 'Belle Epoque'; 'an aaliyah' at Susan Hobbs Gallery, Toronto (2006); 'a dancer dances' at Miguel Abreu Gallery, New York (2006);

'the little contemporaries,' in collaboration with choreographer Maria Hassabi, at SculptureCenter and P.S.1 Contemporary Art Center, New York (2006–07); and 'simple agonie' at Sutton Lane, London (2008).

The result was an entirely new installation, which did not include actual objects from previous exhibitions, but rather drew on Lyall's computer files from those exhibitions. Lyall's working method begins with the interface of the computer. His process involves graphic imaging software, which allows a project to be developed independent of an actual exhibition space. When an opportunity arises Lyall draws on a file to output and fabricate two- and three-dimensional forms and also map them onto the exhibition space. This means that a work exists as information in a file, regardless of whether it has an outing in the form of an exhibition. It also means that, when outputted, a work can, like a musical score, be configured differently, in terms of scale, material used and its interaction with an actual space. This is true for THE POWER BALL and its retrospective referencing of previous exhibitions. By exposing the dichotomies that arise from our understanding of the gallery as a site for presentation, THE POWER BALL investigates how art works can be finite and infinite, and how an "art exhibition" can possess symbolic and imaginary functions.

Like many artists before him, Lyall is interested in the intersection between art and life. This becomes apparent from the moment the installation's title is encountered, with its overlapping of the words "power" and "color" as an alternate qualifier for the word "ball." The title is thereby rendered unpronounceable. Read according to its alternates, though, we find references to both power ball and color ball. The first reading for Toronto-based visitors alluded to the "Power Ball," the annual fundraising gala party of The Power Plant, the highest profile exemplar of the interconnections between the gallery and the worlds of finance, advertising, fashion and entertainment. This reading was reinforced for visitors through the Cinderella-like society figure used to promote the exhibition and also on entering the installation, which included rotating party lights, a fog machine and assembled catering props. With no actual party in action the effect for the viewer was the suggestion of a moment in time, either pre- or post-event—essentially, a party without guests. The second reading "Color Ball" refers to the color-sphere selector used in most computer imaging software. This diagram takes the form of a sphere to incorporate every hue at every intensity and shade, resulting in a grey centre. In notes for the exhibition Lyall suggested that the "Color Ball" is therefore the figure of "every image, whatever." This reading brings art back into the frame. It alludes to the installation both as an image and a collection of images. The interaction of these two very distinct references in the title leads to a third reading. "Power" does not completely eclipse "color" and vice-versa, suggesting through the force of compression an interconnection, but ultimately a distinction between these signifiers of art and life.

Such compressions and distinctions carry through into the installation as if a party and an exhibition were about to merge. On the one hand Lyall's work exuded a sense of pathos concerning the current semiotic preconditions that underpin the exhibition as framing device; on the other it reveled in the possibility of slippage between different representational orders, including traditionally distinct art mediums and moments in art history, as well as stage sets, architectural supports, window dressing and props for a party. The multi-directionality of the slippage meant that the installation could not be read solely as the preparations for, or remnants of, a party. The central armatures of the show were his trademark forms made from alternating sheets of MDF board and Styrofoam. Too low to be read as serving tables, they were more reminiscent of theatrical props or minimalist sculpture. Arranged with obvious intentionality, they served to lead the eye to various points in the space and to choreograph the viewer's movement through the installation. In this way Lyall positioned sculpture and the space of the exhibition as one of potential enactment, which lent his work a provisional rather than finite quality. On walking into the installation, the viewer activated it, but could never complete it.

The slippage between the experience of entering an image, a still life frozen in time, and that of entering a space activated by shifting sunlight, moving spotlights seen through fog and the movement of the viewer through the space, conjured the sense of the installation as a haunted ballroom. Phantasms included the absent guests, the absent artist, references to previous Lyall exhibitions, as well as references to a history of artworks which take social spaces, party events, receptions and celebration as their central theme. These ranged from Marc Camille Chaimowicz's *Celebration? Real Life* (1972) to Judy Chicago's *The Dinner Party* (1974–79) and Rirkrit Tiravanija's work involving food served to visitors and passersby. Other influences Lyall drew upon during his conception of THE POWER BALL include popular films such as *Death Takes a Holiday* (with its remake *Meet Joe Black*), *Dogville* and the fairy tale *Cinderella*. Taking the installation as a whole image, a further reference was the tradition of still-life painting with Lyall paying particular attention to Chardin's tablecloth compositions.

On this level the installation structured the viewers sense of déjà vu in order to articulate and define aspects of the contemporary moment. If, within the installation, the deployment of elements alluded to generalized art historical moments, from the arrangement of shapes as abstract forms through to the idea of the readymade, it also relied on other levels of the familiar. In his SITE Santa Fe installation, Lyall's use of the RE/MAX logo is not simply a quoting or repetition of past artistic strategies, such as when Warhol positioned the red, white and blue-branded Brillo box as art. Rather Lyall relies on the viewer's familiarity with the now frequent slippage between art and commerce to situate a threshold image within the context of a broader installation. Similarly, while recalling Duchamp, the plate stacker in THE POWER BALL is not simply positioned as an object for transcendent contemplation indifferent to its function. It is also positioned in terms of its function by relying on the viewer's familiarity with seeing catering orders, wine glasses and plate stackers within the current context of art museums.

Much of the exhibition's performative and conceptual aspects operated at the level of threshold, often extending well beyond the exhibition space out into the world of institutional promotion. This included the Cinderella-like image, drawn from fashion photography and overlaid with the title, used to market the show. It also included the multiple artwork produced by Lyall for The Power Plant and Partners in Art to help support the exhibition's production. Produced in an edition of 100 and titled *Seul (Alone)* (2008) the work is a hand-blown glass ball containing bath salts and pigment, that if used would stain the body. It is simultaneously a party gift and an artwork that relies on the potential performative agency of the viewer. There was also the performance by artist Ei Arakawa that took place within the installation on the closing weekend, that dramatically reorganized the material elements of the installation, even to the extent of unwrapping stemware and offering viewers water. While ostensibly a discreet work by Arakawa, it operated within the broader context of Lyall's installation, offering a literal closing event but not a sense of completion.

At the close of the exhibition many of its elements were repacked ready to be put back into circulation as functional party ware. The sense that the installation was a succession of images is now echoed in the form of this catalogue, offering the possibility of engaging THE POWER BALL as a series of scenes, or an overall event. There is of course knowingness here on the part of Lyall, who from the outset figured the catalogue as a surrogate impacting on the installation as a site of production. For Lyall the catalogue is one component of a project that meditates on the conditions of exhibition making today.

NO PARTY
Robert Linsley

Scott Lyall's exhibition is a representation of a social event, specifically a fundraising party. An accumulation of carefully chosen elements—of "details" in other words—tell the viewer that what they are looking at is a fictional party. Some of these details suggest that the viewer has arrived just before the event, during set-up, others that the event is over and clean up is in progress. The one thing obviously missing is the party itself. Lyall's work is in the great tradition of modern art—it negates meaning and empties its forms; the non-existence of THE POWER BALL is the absence of art itself.

In this work, nothing should be taken literally, including its absences. Actually that is true of all art, but lesser work claims otherwise. The details of party furniture and accessories build in the viewer's mind an event that cannot be literally presented in the gallery. Instead, it appears as a metonymy, as the space of the event. A metonymy is a trope, one of the many kinds of figurative language, of imaginative, non-literal uses of words. There have been many attempts to apply tropes to visual art but there is no consensus about how that is supposed to be done, and that is one of the reasons why I like to use them. A metonymy is a move in space, to something beside or in the vicinity of the object meant. For example we say "Wall Street reacted ... etc." where Wall Street is spatially associated with the brokers or investors.

There is good reason to think that the trope of metonymy has some relevance for Minimalism and installation-based art practices. The way that an installation of the work of Donald Judd, Larry Bell or Sol LeWitt, for example, resembles the architecture surrounding the urban gallery suggests that it substitutes the expected content of art, namely a human presence, by the gridded city space, meaning both the streets and the high-rise steel and glass buildings. The missing human element is then implied as the people who built and use the city. A metalepsis, a more complex trope, is a metonymy of a metonymy, and it could serve as a useful description of how an artist places themselves in relation to their precursors. Typically, a metalepsis stresses both past and future at the expense of present experience, just as we see in Lyall's installation.[1]

---

1   According to the distinguished literary critic Harold Bloom: "We can define metalepsis as the trope of a trope, the metonymic substitution of a word for a word already figurative. More broadly, a metalepsis or transumption is a scheme, frequently allusive, that refers the reader back to any previous figurative scheme ... In a metalepsis a word is substituted metonymically for a word in a previous trope, so that a metalepsis can be called, maddeningly but accurately, a metonymy of a metonymy ... [it] tends to be either a projection and distancing of the future and so an introjection of the past, by substituting late words for early words in previous tropes, or else more often a distancing and projection of the past and an introjection of the future, by substituting early words for late words in a precursor's tropes. Either way the present vanishes ... (emphasis added)"

Lyall's piece contains another absence at its centre, although it is not immediately apparent as such, namely the generic "sculpture" made of wafers of MDF and pink Styrofoam. The notion of a generic artwork is a very difficult one to realize. It lies behind much art of the eighties, including what was known as "bad" painting, "appropriation art," and newer uses of the readymade, but it was never presented directly as such, rather indirectly as a critique of style or of authorship. The difficulty lies in the fact that a thoroughgoing demonstration of the generic nature of art has no claim to exhibition value. The typical, undistinguished artwork has to be presented in some distinctive way to command our interest, otherwise the art of furniture showrooms would be continuous with that of the museum. To bear down directly on this condition is a mistake that an art student might make, but the mistake of course lies in the abstractness of the idea. Lyall avoids trafficking in art historical or critical generalities, but he teeters on the brink between the concrete generality of minimalism and the abstract notion of a generic art. This is a risky balancing act. The question is whether the work can dispense either with the fictional party or with the central "sculpture." Lyall's stake is that he needs both, and if he can convince us of that he will have achieved what modernism has always tried to achieve, the illusion of aesthetic necessity. The sculpture without the surrounding installation would leave us with an abstract notion of generic art; uninteresting because it is not news in any way. The party installation without the sculpture as a placeholder for art, for the absence at the work's core, would put Lyall's work within a range of well-known practices that bring into question the distinction between art and non-art. Ilya Kabakov, Peter Fishli and David Weiss, and Guillaume Bijl come to mind as practitioners of what is sometimes called "total installation." Clearly Lyall is too ambitious to accept either of these limited positions, yet in this work the details are everything, and slow contemplation of those details gives many pleasures, not the least of which is the familiar but still pleasant experience of not knowing for certain what is and is not intended, even what is meant to be included and what is not.[2]

---

2   The wafer structure of alternating MDF and Styrofoam seems to be an instance of minimalist seriality, but it is also a literalization of the metaleptic substitution of before and after endlessly repeated. Perhaps a metalepsis presumes time as a sandwich, in which the past and the future bracket each other off. In any case, I believe that however pretty they may be their inertness and vacuity is crucial. They work as "cuts" in the exhibition space, even though they don't cut but rather "fill." As such they could be seen as precise inversions of the exemplary openings of Gordon Matta-Clark.

Yet some of the details feel arbitrary; the installation does not hang entirely on its central absence. In historical art the unmotivated detail was always something that exceeded the demands of the work, a surplus of energy, of excitement, of expression, hence the very definition of beauty. Abstraction always took a hard line with the detail, but the kind of abstract painting that is built around absences and negations has not only tended to eliminate details but to move toward the generic detail. In a counter move, "total installation," which aims to duplicate the world of ordinary things, accumulates a million specificities to create a general impression or to convey an abstract idea. Lyall refuses this collapsed dialectic, which from both directions simply affirms the given—our world of abstractions and generic products—and sticks to an older idea that the aesthetic value of the concrete detail lies in its necessity within the whole, and that the beauty of the detail—its value for us—lies in its escape from that necessity.

Décor

To understand where Lyall's work belongs in the panorama of contemporary art we must draw some distinctions within the very rich field of "installation." I would like to single out some important installations made by Marcel Broodthaers, particularly *Un Jardin d'Hiver* of 1974 and *Décor* at the Institute of Contemporary Arts in London the following year. The latter piece has been discussed as a critique of Belgian colonialism, and of the continuation of colonial exploitation by tourism during the postwar period. This may be true, but I would like to point out that these works are also metonymies. Instead of culture they present the place of culture, specifically the public/private world of bourgeois art in its heyday at the turn of the last century; the palm court culture of tea in the conservatory, of late-romantic music, of wealthy American travelers in Europe; the period of Mahler, Bruckner, Hofmannsthal and Strauss in Vienna, of Debussy, Proust, Valéry, Monet and Cézanne in Paris, of Lieberman and Corinth in Berlin, of Henry James in London. This was the pinnacle of bourgeois art. Its audience was sensitive to dissonances and understood and anticipated the transformation of those dissonances into harmonies. Strange sounds and clashing colours, after a period of acclimatization, could be accepted as new and delectable experiences.[3] It was only after World War I that dissonance in art was radicalized and took on a political meaning. Meanwhile, the cannons in Broodthaers' *Décor* are a pathetic sight in the era of total

---

3   Dissonance means precisely the relation between part and whole, because it is the unwillingness of a chosen detail, a particular sound or note, to play the part demanded of it within the harmonic whole.

war, almost a sentimental one. They suggest a painting by Henri Rousseau of dignitaries in bemedalled uniforms. The chairs in *Un Jardin d'Hiver* might come from Manet's *Concert in the Tuileries: Music in the Tulleries Gardens* (1862), although that work is from an earlier period, it captures the social milieu of the art that emerged from and formed modern taste, a milieu now lost, only recapturable as an irony.

I suggested earlier that Lyall's work, because of the way that it negates the present, is a metalepsis. If this is so then it should accomplish another metonymic displacement, to *the place of the place* of culture. For the culture-critical installation artists of the 1960s and 1970s *that* place was the economy. It was no longer enough to indicate the architectural context of art, the social relations that circulate there had to be acknowledged. It is significant that Lyall's teacher at CalArts, Michael Asher, sits on the cusp of this development. He accepts Carl Andre's concept of sculpture as place and pushes it to the point where it begins to irritate the institution, but not as far as an outright confrontation with the social interests that inhabit it. Asher remains an artist at the limit of self-critique, his practice doesn't move over the line into social intervention, or direct work on the framing conditions of art. But in any case we know now that political gestures in art serve an aesthetic function, and that is their political value. A later generation of Lyall's contemporaries, including figures such as Francis Alÿs, Jeremy Deller, Teresa Margolles, Gillian Wearing and Rirkrit Tiravanija, has accepted this limit. Tiravanija is known for work that produces a community in the gallery, but the others have moved their practice out of the art milieu to work with subcultures or various self-identified social groups. Their work with these groups comes back into art as an image, so they extend the materials of art but don't at all break out of the realm of semblance. Some of these artists leave behind a gallery installation or a video as a souvenir of a performance or event, and in this respect Lyall's piece has to be seen in the context of what is today called relational aesthetics, but only to emphasize how he stands apart from this now canonical mode. The practitioners of relational aesthetics in effect claim that there is not one place of culture, but many places, their metonymy of a work such as Broodthaers' *Décor* is to find the place of the place of culture in social discourse, in a creative community, with the recognition that any community has the potential to alter the conditions of life, at least locally. The "communities" that these artists invoke are themselves really just further tropes of the 1960s notions of culture as place. This is in line with Lyall's practice, but his metalepsis is stronger, more compelling, and less idealist, he finds the place of the place of culture to be a void.

If Broodthaers presents the place of culture today as a touristic hell, and clearly points to its derivation in a *fin de siècle* bourgeois society that now appears exactly the opposite of what it imagined itself to be, if not vulgar then utterly naive, Lyall says that the real place of culture is no place at all. For him this absent sociality is itself a substitution for (a troping of) the work space, which is exactly the infinitesimal gap between the two phrases that constitute the installation's title, literally produced by Lyall on the computer in his studio. This is Lyall's version of the Mallarméan *néant*[4] that is the productive heart of all sublime gaming with harmony and dissonance. It's significant that Broodthaers himself believed that Mallarmé was "the founder of contemporary art." He metonymized his predecessor's transformation of words into images by placing objects adjacent to signs, and further metonymized Mallarmé's spatialization of language by constructing two fictional narrative spaces, the *Musée d'art Moderne, Département des Aigles* (1970–71) and the installations which he placed under the collective title of *Décor*, both of which present the place of culture rather than art itself. Lyall's metalepsis of Broodthaers, his shift to the "place of the place" of culture, posits a continuity from the symbolism of the fin de siècle to the Pop/Minimalism nexus of the 1960s.[5] But this is not just an art historical insight; it is a perspective founded on the realization that the neo-Pop of the 1980s, now a dominant position in the market, together with the more recent relational aesthetics, prove that neither pop nor conceptualist practices found a "real" context outside of the aesthetic. The scandal of Lyall's work lies in its implicit negation of the claim of relational aesthetics to have found that social "real" in sub-cultural communities that in fact are only tropes for the community of discourse of contemporary art.[6]

---

4   Lyall tries, in Mallarmé's phrase, to create "sensuous allegories of nothing."

5   In line with the definition of metalepsis laid out in the first note above, Lyall introjects the past, meaning that he takes *fin de siècle* aestheticism to be his own flaw, not just the obsolete ideology of the age of art for art's sake, and projects the future, meaning that the social ideal of peers such as Tiravanija, a community of creative discourse as an image of a humane society, is distanced into a mere image and then subjected to the standards of art. In a word, art will be the horizon of the dream of an incrementally improved social order, and by art we mean properly nihilistic modernism.

6   There is a sense in which Lyall has also performed a metalepsis on Asher's work. It is clear to me now, as it was never before, that Asher's relocation of a statue of George Washington from the front of the Art Institute of Chicago into one of its 18th century galleries is exactly a memorialized, or marmorealized, "party" in the same sense as Lyall's installation. The guest is absent, actually dead, and the ongoing party is the tradition of art, the voices and movements, real, metaphorical and represented, of the pictures on the walls. Asher's piece is a witness to the petrification of whatever might once have been the "life" of the art world. Lyall has not been "influenced" by his teacher, rather he has effected a radical repositioning of his predecessor's practice, which now, for me at least, can only be seen in the light of the later work. This is exactly the transposition of early and late that metalepsis aims to produce.

However self-referential it may be, if by self-referential we also mean historically aware, and utterly self-aware of its own grounding in a history of modern art, Lyall's work is not art about art. It takes what I believe to be the most radically progressive and politically efficacious position any art today can take; namely that modernism is not a self-critical practice that reflects on its own conditions, but fundamentally a negation of meaning. Techniques of self-criticism and self-analysis are to serve this more basic drive. The perspectives we need to understand this, from Mallarmé to Broodthaers to Lyall, are provided by literature. Lyall is a literary artist in the same sense that Robert Smithson and Broodthaers were literary artists; he doesn't have to use words or narratives in his work, though he might, but he understands the literariness of the modernist claim to material presence. He understands that the material "facts" of any work are not to be taken as merely such, but he also avoids the trap of promulgating social and political ideals. Art must be de-idealized, as must be our social relations. From this perspective, Lyall's installation demands more from its viewers, and proposes a more difficult role for art, than do those of his colleagues such as Tiravanija, or Deller. Meaning is not so easily come by, and good intentions are not so confidently proclaimed.

But the most surprising and inventive aspect of the show is the way that Lyall reintroduces the present. The windows of The Power Plant, long closed off by the walls normally used to display art, have been reopened, and the daylight outside the gallery allowed to mingle with the artificial light of the exhibition, itself carefully orchestrated to signify a party. The blinds are not opened very much, so the effect is quite subtle, and the more beautifully so. I think that we have all, at some special moments, vividly experienced the effect of simultaneous daylight and artificial light, and it is a powerful device to heighten the sense of time. When clock time and sun time come into close proximity this nearness makes us strongly aware of our own present. With a simple gesture Lyall restores immediate experience to the metaleptic voiding of the present characteristic of any artist's difficult but productive relations with his or her predecessors, and he does it in a typically avant-gardist manner, as ordinary time and ordinary life. Like any neo-Dada artist post-1960, here Lyall seems to want to do away with the referentiality and allusiveness of ambitious modern art, which keeps it tied to its past the more strenuously it embraces the new, in favour of the simple life, the here and now as fulfilled, real, not in need of any aesthetic supplement or compensation. But then one has to take pause and remember that neo-Dada performance is one of the sources for the socially engaged installations that form Lyall's immediate context, so perhaps history is not easily dodged. I believe it is crucial that the alienated, solitary viewing experience, which will be present anyway, in all installations, however strident the efforts to call over that gap, be allowed one utopian moment—one gleam or sunbeam of the possibility of a fulfilled present outside of art.[7] Lyall puts perspective on this materialist utopia by making it the third important element in the show. The entire exhibition then becomes metonymic; artwork (the fills), party installation and life all stand adjacent. There is no metaphoric substitution of art for life or life for art, and the middle term, the party installation, is relieved of any ambition to perform a sublation of the two. His insight that an aesthetic emptiness will fall between all individual stances, and that the community will be a community of distinctions finally unable to constitute itself as a coherent whole, is a remarkable act of continuity with modernism that emerges directly from the heart of its antagonist, the critical avant-garde.

Unlike music and literature, visual art has to accomplish all its goals through the dimensions of space, and so its greatest achievement is to make time more vivid. This is also the burden of Proust's magnificent novel *Remembrance of Things Past*, which is constructed around a series of social gatherings. At the final set piece in the book, the Guermantes ball, the narrator Marcel forgets for a moment that time has passed and the people he has known all his life have aged. He steps into the drawing room and has the uncanny impression that the guests are all in fancy dress, that they are only pretending to be old. What follows is veritable paradigm of metalepsis as present experience offers a heightened awareness of all the lost pasts and futures, meaning above all past and future art:

> ... a party like this at which I found myself was something much more valuable
> than an image of the past: it offered me as it were all the successive images—
> which I had never seen—which separated the past from the present, better

---

7   Where Benjamin H.D. Buchloh wants to build a tradition from Rodchenko's reading room, through Duchamp's surrealist installations to Broodthaers and Asher as a tradition of cultural critique, Lyall has taught me that the greater tradition goes directly from the culture of the *fin de siècle*, through Duchamp to Asher and Broodthaers and now Lyall as a refusal of what passes for politics in favour of aesthetic negation as the strongest modern political position. As is well known, Buchloh is one of Broodthaers' best critics. With respect to the present argument, it is significant that he has acknowledged Broodthaers' metonymy of literature, and his metalepsis: "Broodthaers speaks in old-fashioned art terms to a viewer expecting the modernist idiom." All great art may well have a retrospective quality, which will appear to some as a paradoxically conservative streak.

still it showed me the relationship that existed between the present and the
past; it was like an old-fashioned peepshow of the years, the vision not of a
moment but of a person situated in the disturbing perspective of Time.

In Lyall's piece the person caught in temporal perspective is the viewer, so in a sense
the piece contains another absence, that of the subject. That is to say, there is neither
fictional character to animate the scene, nor artist to do the same.

Robert Linsley is a Canadian artist and widely published writer.

RESPONSE: THE POWER BALL / EI ARAKAWA

Caroline Busta

In Scott Lyall's THE POWER BALL power was displaced and constituted only through a collective performance. Entering the installation from a darkened corridor was to emerge stage right into a performance in progress. Lighting suspended from theater rigging cast spots—some gelled, others oscillating—throughout the gallery's 3,655 square foot space. Around the room, Lyall had positioned several plinths of MDF and Styrofoam loosely arranged as an equilateral triangle set amid an odd collection of semi-unpacked catering supplies and decorations. The overall composition evoked a sense of backstage, but a staged sense of backstage, as the roving spotlights dramatized crates of still-wrapped stemware, haphazardly aligned crowd stanchions, and wreaths of dried flowers waiting to be rearranged. It was the exoskeleton of a spectacle—a party suspended and abandoned just as the market crashed last September—neither exactly its aftermath nor its untouched preparations. And standing on such a stage, the intercalated viewer was neither the performer nor the spectator, neither the entertaining talent nor the paying guest.

This mutable role of Lyall's viewer is, perhaps, similar to the viewer of reality television who is both outside and inside the spectacle, an observer given "exclusive," behind-the-scenes access to the staging of a pseudo-democratic competition to become famous. Spatial binaries such as backstage and on-stage are ruptured while social ones, such as pedestrian and celebrity, are destabilized. As in Judy Chicago's *The Dinner Party* (1974–79), Lyall adds a third side to the dinner table; a supernumerary alternative that is not one or the other, but representative of everything that is beyond the first two. In an auxiliary text accompanying this show Lyall quoted Duchamp writing, "One is unity, two is the double, and three is the rest."

Eluding the given duality of institution and artist, Lyall often engages a third party in making his work. For example, in executing his contribution to SITE Santa Fe's Seventh International Biennial in 2008, Lyall asked a group of local muralists to supply the image content. This collaborative impulse should not be mistaken, however, for a "relational" demonstration of sociability or democracy. If anything, Lyall incorporates an "other" to generate a layer of abstraction, a way of obfuscating translation, and leading to alternative readings beyond those he may have initially intended. At The Power Plant, Lyall called on the New York-based artist Ei Arakawa. Known for staging decentralized, carnivalesque performances, Arakawa was invited by Lyall to make use of the exhibition's material elements, physical space and closing weekend to stage a work of his own. In making this offer to Arakawa, Lyall was not interested in eliciting a collaboration that would reinforce the exhibition's themes. Rather, the exchange would hinge on the exhibition's materials. To borrow from Bernadette Corporation's recent screenplay *Eine Pinot Grigio, Bitte,* "The medium is what we have in common, our common situation" and through it, an obligation to "the production of subjectivity/society/space."

Prior to the performance, Lyall provided Arakawa with a listing of materials that would be on hand. While the installation's overarching conceit may have been an institutional gala, Lyall had inserted a layer of subjective detail among the catering materials. On what reads like the prep-sheet of a party planner who's cracked, it is stated that a "photo of two half-naked women in a bathroom stall can be seen through the plastic wrap [securing the crates of plates], one of the girls holding the other's hair back as she vomits." And, visible text—as though concrete poetry or the directives of a Dada diagram— includes "GOD JUL," "MADE IN POLAND" and "EXCLUSIVE AFFAIR RENTALS," repeatedly.

With this information in hand and these materials at his disposal, Arakawa called on eight people already familiar with Lyall's work—among them, previous collaborators such as Rachel Harrison, Sam Lewitt and Blake Rayne—to each choose a scene from a film to be shown during the performance.[1] The selection, which ranged from the communards' celebration in Peter Watkins's *La Commune (Paris, 1871)* to the final denouement/explosion of Michelangelo Antonioni's *Zabriskie Point,* would be projected within the gallery on a screen that would be both constructed and dismantled during the performance. From there, Arakawa drafted a loose score. With the exception of a few electronics, tools and a wooden frame bisecting the gallery, he drew all resources from Lyall's installation: tables were unfolded and stacked to serve as scaffolding; tablecloths stretched out and tacked to the frame became the screen; plates were unpacked; silverware was arranged, and alongside the desultory decorations, laid out across the MDF and Styrofoam plinths; water was boiled to fill stemware handed out on trays. The plinths carried television monitors that the "caterer" performers tuned. More than directing people, Arakawa choreographed the elements of Lyall's set. Over the course of a Fantasia-like hour, these efforts brought Lyall's piece to its anticipated climax: A party was thrown. Guests convened. Glasses broke. And spectators, framing bits of action with iPhone cameras, (perhaps unwittingly) erased the proscenium, becoming part of the performance.

Of course, in a sense there never had been any proscenium, neither for Arakawa's stage, nor for Lyall's. When Arakawa built the screen, he located it centrally, bisecting the space, but not so much to divide as to de-centre. Dressed in projection, the centre dissolved into the illusionary space of the films. And as the projection surface was built and dismantled over the course of the performance, the image plane fluctuated, traveling from gallery wall to scaffolding to tablecloth to passersby. In washing the components of Lyall's THE POWER BALL with the image-content of the films, the set was illuminated with light from the projector—one shade of spectacle projected onto another, one stage set, with only a slight shift of meaning, becoming the next scene. Also included among the elements of Lyall's installation, and retained for Arakawa's performance was the sculpture of an owl, the kind found in suburban gardens. As Hegel wrote and the Situationists maintained, "When philosophy paints its grey in grey, one form of life has become old, and by means of grey it cannot be rejuvenated, but only known. The owl of Minerva, takes its flight only when the shades of night are gathering."

---

1 The program of films comprised the following:
Peter Watkins *La Commune (Paris, 1871)* (the communards' celebration)
Dieterle/Reinhardt *A Midsummer Night's Dream* (whirl conducted by Puck)
Paul Verhoeven *Showgirls* (nightclub act)
Hans-Jürgen Syberberg *Parsifal* (lament after Kundry)
Morton DaCosta *Auntie Mame* (decoration of Beekman Place)
Michelangelo Antonioni *Zabriskie Point* (denouement/explosions)
Alan Pakula *The Parallax View* (convention centre assassination)
Claire Denis *Beau travail* (private disco with mirror slats)
Lars von Trier *Dogville* (destruction of Dogville: "they did not meet my standards")

Caroline Busta is a writer and assistant editor for Artforum magazine.

AN ACKNOWLEDGEMENT: JUDY CHICAGO AND MARC CAMILLE CHAIMOWICZ

Scott Lyall

*The Moon has gone down
And so the Pleiades, it is the middle
of the night, the hour passes,
and I am alone in bed.*

— Sappho, (fragment, around 580 B.C.E.)

There are scholars who claim to know that it is springtime in this poem, because that is when the Moon sets before midnight in the Aegean. And it is even early spring, because the Pleiades—a cluster of stars whose name means "many"—have also fallen before the middle of the night. It is spring, but without brightness; an early spring with not-one colour. "The hour passes": and there is an "I"—first person singular—alone in bed.

"The hour passes": a good description of the subject of my show.

Sappho's poem is a lyric: words where previously there was sentiment. "Wo est war," as Freud said: "Where It was, [an] I shall be." And if the "It" here is a reference to the object-cause of sentiment—of blind demands, unspeakable needs, passionate attachments and satisfactions—then the "I" which supersedes it pertains to two distinctive functions. It is the ego—that which specifies and gentrifies its own pleasures; and it is the generic point at which someone is exactly the same as everyone else. With "I", we have the imagination of what is either one or multiple, either a poet alone in bed or a choral dispersal, an unknown audience. *I is an other* (Rimbaud wrote): I is multiple and generic; and I is embedded with bawdy delicacy as the singular voice of poetry. Or else: an I, wrote Emily Dickinson, could be a letter sent to the world. "Je somme," Orlan declared at a lecture in Toronto. It makes sense, then, that the light that has had to pass away in the poem—the light whose disappearance proposes the subject as somehow subtracted from visuality—was made of starlight (a cluster of many) as well as the Moon (a single refraction). The hour passes *between states* in which the one relates to multiples. It stands for neither, though. It is a gap between two pairs, two one-and-others. It is the phrasing of empty enjoyment between a nightfall and its audience. There is an hour, without aurality—regardless of every image we have of it—when art is content to converse solely with such an oscillating con-foundation.

What passes by this hour, between the composer and the starlight? What transpires between the moon and all of the equivalent letter-I's? The writer Cornelius Castoriadis proposed a succession of partial answers without emphasizing any one of them as the key to what is happening. English readers interpret "hour" as a standard measure of clock time, so what passes for them in the poem is a piece of the working day. But this word appears where classical Greek could have also chosen *hora*, a word that points to a seasonal allegory: here it is springtime, as we said. To the mechanics of daily clock time we add this other temporality: the passing season as the section of a dilated, symbolic time. And then again, the *hora of something* is when it is experienced as at its prime, when it is truly fine and full, when it could fulgurate, when it is *ready*. (The time scale shifts again, to that of replete but ephemeral presence, impressing the smallest jolts of infinity into the clock and the rolling cycle.) In the *Symposium*, Alcibiades recalled an evening when as a boy he desired to be called upon (singled out, seduced, celebrated) by Socrates. He said he entered the teacher's mantle, but then awoke in the morning only to find he had slept comfortably, untouched throughout the night. He concluded by way of complaint: "The teacher offends. He scorned my *hora*. He spurned my youth and ignored my beauty. The master *left me alone in bed.*"

There is a final meaning: the *hora* is one's appointed hour to die. (In Greek mythology the *Horae* composed a half-sisterhood with the Fates.) The hour passing, then, is a brace against the cut of these fatalities. It is the realization that something—your inexistence?—is behind you. So, "like a freed convict," surviving both her information and sentence, the *horal* poet deposes a world where what is inevitable dissolves behind her. And "[t]he light that rains down [...] is that of the dawn following [...] judgment. The life that begins that day on earth—when the hour passes—is called humanity."[1]

Thus, the hour is a compression and a *millefeuille* of layers and cuts. The word is constant, but it is threaded by subtle shifts of state and scale. It is stillness as well as passage. It is subtraction as an event. The central themes are inconsistencies: sensuous-emptying-satiation. And if we keep these facts in mind, we can wager a second poetic (mis)reading, whose syntactical ricketiness I also endorse as very important to my own goals:

The Moon and the many stars
have all gone down, it is the middle
of the [night-season-hour-coming of spring-blossom of youth-hour of death] are all departed,
and I am alone in bed.

---

1 Giorgio Agamben, *The Coming Community,* trans. Michael Hardt, University of Minnesota Press: Minneapolis, 1993).

SCOTT LYALL

Born in Toronto, Ontario, 1964
Lives and works in Toronto

EDUCATION

1987   Queen's University, Kingston
1990   LL.B University of Toronto
1993   MFA, California Institute of the Arts, Valencia

SOLO/COLLABORATIVE EXHIBITIONS

2009   'Scott Lyall,' Miguel Abreu Gallery, New York
2008   'Scott Lyall: The Color Ball,' The Power Plant, Toronto
2008   'simple agony,' Sutton Lane, London
2007   'the little contemporaries,' Sculpture Center, Long Island City
2007   'Gloria' (collaboration with Maria Hassabi), The Ballroom, Marfa; PS 122, New York
2006   'a dancer dances,' Miguel Abreu Gallery, New York
2006   'When Hangover Becomes Form' (collaboration with Rachel Harrison), Contemporary Art Gallery, Vancouver; LACE, Los Angeles
2006   'an aaliyah,' Susan Hobbs Gallery, Toronto
2004   'The Canon Copiers,' Susan Hobbs Gallery, Toronto
2002   'OK!ahoma (2000-2002)', Art Gallery of York University, Toronto
2001   'Scott Lyall,' Susan Hobbs Gallery, Toronto
2001   'Scott Lyall/Josh Blackwell,' Goldman/Tevis, Los Angeles
1997-98 'Washington Square,' Greene Naftali Gallery, New York
1996   'Scott Lyall: Plugged and Unplugged,' Greene Naftali Gallery, New York
1994   'Scott Lyall/Blake Rayne,' John Goode Gallery, New York

GROUP EXHIBITIONS

2009   'Breaking New Ground Underground,' Stonescape, Calistoga, California
2009   'Practice vs. Object,' organized by Margaret Liu Clinton, Miguel Abreu Gallery, New York
2009   'Collatéral,' Le Confort Moderne, Poitiers, France
2009   'The Lining of Forgetting,' curated by Xandra Eden, Austin Museum of Art, Austin, Texas
2009   'CODE SHARE: 5 continents, 10 biennials, 20 artists, curated by Simon Rees, Contemporary Art Centre (SMC/CAC), Vilnius, Lithuania
2008   'Lucky Number 7: The 7th SITE Santa Fe International Biennial,' curated by Lance M. Fung, SITE Santa Fe
2008   'The Lining of Forgetting,' Weatherspoon Art Museum, Greensboro
2007   'Regroup Show,' Miguel Abreu Gallery, New York
2007   'Group,' Sutton Lane c/o Ghislaine Hussenot, Paris
2007   'Massiv Analog Academy,' curated by Gareth James and John Kelsey, Galerie Christian Nagel, Cologne
2007   'For the People of Paris,' Sutton Lane c/o Ghislaine Hussenot, Paris
2006   'Hands Up/Hand Down,' Miguel Abreu Gallery, New York
2006   'We Can Do This Now,' The Power Plant, Toronto
2004   'Yarns,' Rubin Gallery, Seattle
2004   'Scott Lyall, Roe Ethridge, Blake Rayne,' Greener Pastures, Toronto
2003   'Psychotopes,' YYZ Artist's Outlet, Toronto
2003   'Scott Lyall, Brandon Latau, Cory McCorkle,' Mary Goldman Gallery, Los Angeles
2000   'New York Projects,' Delfina, London
1999   'Construction Drawings, curated by Klaus Biesenbach, Kunst Werke, Berlin
1998   'Construction Drawings, P.S.1 Contemporary Art Center, Long Island City
1998   'Architecture! Architecture! Architecture!,' Hunter College Times Square Gallery, New York
1998   'E PLURALUS NIHIL,' organized by Colin DeLand, American Fine Arts Co., New York
1995   'ReZone,' Diverse Works Gallery, Houston
1995   'Club Berlin', Kunstshaft Site, 46th Venice Biennale
1993   'The Los Angeles Thing,' ICA, London; Glasgow College of Art, Glasgow
1993   '04/30/1993,' Rainforest Apartments, Hollywood
1993   'Real, Post, Other,' The Municipal Building, Los Angeles

BIBLIOGRAPHY

Adler, Dan, 'Scott Lyall: The Power Plant, Toronto,' *Artforum*, January 2009

Adler, Dan 'When Hangover Becomes Form,' exhibition essay, Contemporary Art Gallery, Vancouver

Adler, Dan, 'Scott Lyall: Susan Hobbs Gallery,' *Zing Magazine*, No. 177, 2002, pp.249-250.

Antonova, Iliana, 'Best of 2008: Scott Lyall, The Color Ball,' *SNAP! Magazine*, Vol. 4, December 2008

Ayerza, Josefina, ed., 'Profane Illuminations,' *Lacanian Ink 28*, November, 2006 (illustration)

Ballengee, Brian, et al. 'Mob Rule #9, Sacred Cows and Dead Horses,' *NY Arts Magazine*, February-March 1998, pp.6-7

Carson, Andrea, 'Scott Lyall: The Power Plant,' *ARTnews*, December, 2008, p. 134.

Bonham-Carter, Charlotte, 'Stuck On You,' *ArtReview*, June 2006, p.25

Chisholm, Christie, 'Come Out and Play,' *Alibi New Mexico*, v. 17 no. 27, 3-9 July, 2008

Dault, Gary Michael, 'Scott Lyall at Susan Hobbs,'
    The Globe and Mail, January 5, 2002

Eden, Xandra, 'Scott Lyall, Susan Hobbs Gallery,'
    Canadian Art, Summer 2004, pp. 92-93

Edwards, Thomas, 'Artists Work to Redefine their
    Spaces,' *The Houston Post*, March 6, 1995

Fairfield, Douglas, 'SITE' out of Luck,' *Santa Fe New
    Mexican*, July 31, 2008

Goddard , Peter, 'Stocks Dive, Art Show Thrives,'
    The Toronto Star, September 27, 2008

Goddard, Peter, 'An Uncertain Approach,' *The Toronto
    Star*, June 19, 2008

Goddard, Peter, 'Take a Walk on the Smelly Side,' *The
    Toronto Star*, April 1, 2006

Gookin, Kirby and Khan, Robin, eds., *Promotional Copy*,
    New York, 1993

Gopnik, Blake, 'Best of 2008,' *The Washington Post*,
    December 28, 2008

Gopnik, Blake, 'A Site for Thinking Outside the Box,'
    The Washington Post, July 6, 2008

Greene, David A., 'Scott Lyall, Greene Naftali Gallery,'
    Frieze, No. 39, March-April 1998, pp. 88-89

Hamilton, Emily Eliza, 'The High Concept No
    Concept Art Show,' *Mass Art Guide*, April, 2006

Hanna, Deirdre, 'Random Reason,' *NOW Magazine*,
    January 3-9, 2002

Higgs, Matthew, 'On the Ground: New York,' *Artforum*,
    December, 2006 (illustration)

Ichihiri, Kentaro, 'I am going around the world...,' *BT
    Tokyo*, June, 2006

Lyall, Scott, 'simple agonie,' in Isaac, Jay and Romano,
    Tony, eds., *Hunter and Cook*, Vol. 2, February,
    2009

Lyall, Scott, 'lecture to accompany the consumption
    of a multiple,' in Rowlands, Alun and Williams,
    Matt, eds., *Novel*, Anna Catherina
    Bibliothekswohnung, October-November, 2008

Lyall, Scott, 'The Episcene', in James, Gareth, Lewitt,
    Sam, and Tompson, Cheyney, eds., *Scorched
    Earth*, (November, 2006, forthcoming)

Mahovsky, Trevor, 'Rachel Harrison and Scott Lyall,'
    Artforum, May 2006

Matotek, Jennifer, 'Focus: Scott Lyall,' *Switch 1:1*, The
    Power Plant, Winter, 2008

Miles, Christopher, 'Part of the Package: Scott Lyall and
    Rachel Harrison Remain True to Themselves,'
    The Los Angeles Times, August 14, 2006

Milroy, Sarah, 'Sweet Ideas, But Do They Hold Up?'
    The Globe and Mail, September 27, 2008

Milroy, Sarah, 'The Idea of a Bright Tomorrow is So
    Yesterday,' *The Globe and Mail*, September 20,
    2008

Milroy, Sarah, 'Critic's Choice: Scott Lyall,' *The Globe
    and Mail*, December 15, 2001

Pedrosa, Adriano, 'Scott Lyall at Greene Naftali,'
    Artforum, June 1998, pp. 135-136

Purchuk, Andrew, 'Critic's Pick,' *Artforum.com*,
    April-May, 2003

Ratman, Neru, 'Gallery Controlled Diet,' *The Face*,
    August 2000

Rattemeyer, Christian, 'Garage heir, Landschaft da,'
    Blitz Review, Summer, 2000

Rinebold, Mary, 'Orchard Underground,' Artnet.com,
    September 6, 2006

Robert, Alison, 'A Brooklyn Cheer for the British Art
    Scene,' *Evening Standard*, August 1, 2000

Rosenberg, Karen, 'Take a Walk on the (Not So Wild)
    Lower East Side,' *New York Magazine*,
    October 2, 2006

Rudd, Claire, 'The Lining of Forgetting: Austin
    Museum of Art,' *Fluent Collaborative*, Issue 24,
    June 2009

Rhodes, Richard, ed., 'The Year in Review: The Top 10
    Exhibitions of 2008,' *Canadian Art*, December 2008
    (<http://www.canadian art.ca)

Rhodes, Richard, ed., 'Toronto Now: The Moment,'
    Canadian Art, Winter 2007, pp 58-59

Schmerler, Sarah, 'Scott Lyall at Miguel Abreu Gallery,'
    Time Out New York, Number 576, October 2006

Schmerler, Sarah, 'Scott Lyall,' *Time Out New York*,
    Number 122, January, 1998, p. 46

Schmitz, Edgar, 'New York projects,' *Kunstforum*,
    November-December 2000, p.48

Schwartz, Jerry, 'New York Journal,' *Modern Painters*,
    November, 2006, p. 58

Servertar, Stuart, 'Scott Lyall: Greene Naftali Gallery,'
    New York Press, February 28, 1996

Tevis, John, 'Yarns,' (exhibition essay), Rubin Gallery,
    Seattle, Fall 2004

Millet, Catherine, ed., 'Exporama,' *Art Press*, February, 1998

EXHIBITION CATALOGUES AND BOOK

Adler, Dan and Lyall, Scott, in Kathleen McLean, ed.,
    Scott Lyall: OKilahoma, (ex cat), Art Gallery of
    York University, Toronto, 2002

Cook, Sarah, Eden, Xandra, and Roberts, John, in Eden,
    Xandra, ed., *The Lining of Forgetting*, (ex cat) The
    Weatherspoon Museum, 2008

Fung, Lance M., and Stewart Heon, Laura, *Lucky
    Number 7, Vols. 1 and 2*, SITE Santa Fe, 2008

Linsley, Robert and Lyall, Scott, *Around the Episcene*, Old
    Mill Books, Vancouver, 2007

Sutton Lane Gallery, *For the People of Paris*, (ex cat),
    January, 2007

THE POWER PLANT

Board of Directors

PRESIDENT
Nancy McCain

VICE-PRESIDENT
Shanitha Kachan

TREASURER
Margaret McNee

BOARD MEMBERS
Paul E. Bain
William J. S. Boyle, C.M.
John Clinton
Michael Cooper

Jean-François Courville
Stéfan Danis
Perry Dellelce
Ted Geatros
Jane Halverson Vendittelli
Kerry Harris
Trinity Jackman
Mark Kingwell
James Lahey
Aaron Latner
Kelly Mark
Liza Mauer
Maya Mavjee
Elisa Nuyten

Laura Rapp
Evan Siddall
Jeff Stober
Victoria Webster

HONOURARY DIRECTORS
Thomas H. Bjarnason
Lonti Ebers
James D. Fleck, O.C.
Victoria Jackman
Phil Lind
Jay Smith

Staff

DIRECTOR
Gregory Burke

SENIOR CURATOR OF PROGRAMS
Helena Reckitt

HEAD OF REGISTRATION,
INSTALLATION & FACILITIES
Paul Zingrone

HEAD OF FINANCE & OPERATIONS/
EXHIBITIONS MANAGER
Christy Thompson

HEAD OF DEVELOPMENT
Sarah Bywater

COORDINATOR, DIRECTOR'S OFFICE
& SPECIAL DEVELOPMENT PROJECTS
Sadaf Virji

SUPPORT SERVICES COORDINATOR
Karen Mitchell

ASSISTANT CURATOR OF EXHIBITIONS
Jennifer Matotek

ASSISTANT CURATOR OF
PUBLIC PROGRAMS
Jon Davies

MAJOR EVENTS & DONOR PROGRAMS
COORDINATOR
Tracy Briggs

MEMBERSHIP & DEVELOPMENT
ASSOCIATE
Angela Grabham

MARKETING & COMMUNICATIONS
COORDINATOR
Robin Boyko

HEAD ANIMATEUR
Daniela Esposito

INTERNS
Linda Chalmers
Stacy Ernst

Katherine Pill
Amy Uyeda

ANIMATEURS
Anna Bouzina
Lyndsey Cope
Sarah Febbraro
Robert Keogh
Rima Puteris
Andrea Raymond
Macy Siu

EXHIBITION INSTALLATION
CREW
Jamie Crane
Jodie James Elliott
Eric Glavin
Eric Goulem
Danielle Greer
Garth Johnson
John Kennedy
Simon McNally
Doug Moore
John Verhaeven

The Power Plant Contemporary Art Gallery is a registered Canadian charitable organization supported by its members, sponsors, donors and funding bodies at all levels of government. We gratefully acknowledge the assistance of the Canada Council for the Arts, the Ontario Arts Council, Toronto Arts Council and Harbourfront Centre.

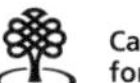

Canada Council for the Arts · Conseil des Arts du Canada   ONTARIO ARTS COUNCIL · CONSEIL DES ARTS DE L'ONTARIO   TORONTO ARTS COUNCIL   Harbourfront centre

PARTNERS IN ART

Partners in Art (PIA) is a non-profit group of Toronto art enthusiasts with an interest in supporting the visual arts in Canada in two ways: first, by partnering with established arts organizations on collaborative fund-raising projects; and second, by furthering members' own understanding and knowledge of the visual arts through an active education program. The group cultivates alliances among artists, dealers, curators, educators, businesses, and the public to develop vital and exciting contemporary art projects that raise the awareness of Canadian art and artists nationally and internationally. PIA was The Power Plant's Commissioning Partner for the gallery's 2008 and 2009 commissions.

Shabin Mohamed and Eleanor Shen, CO-CHAIRS
Tamara Bahry-Paterson, Colette Barber, Mary Bartlett-Keating, Sharon Baruch, Kim Barwise, Nancy Belsher, Kim Bozak, Jane Brisebois, Susan Caskey, Nina Chagnon, Helene Clarkson, Kelly Connacher, Kathleen Crook, Lisa Dinnick, Sarah Dinnick, Heli Donaldson, Dorothy Engelman, Eileen Farrow, Rita Field-Marsham, Angela Feldman, Yvonne Fleck, Patricia Fogler, Leslie Giller, Sharon Graham, Karen Hannaford, Sally Hannon, Jocelyn Hidi, Kathy Houde-Lovas, Linda Jamieson, Judy Jarvis, Mimi Joh, Michelle Koerner, Tiana Koffler Boyman, Barbara Keilhauer, Elske Kofman, Carol Lloyd-Pinnington, Barb Macdonald, Liza Mauer, Susan McArthur, Alison McDonald, Michelle Meneley, Patricia Muir, Julie Norton, Pauline Nowak, Elisa Nuyten, Julia Ouellette, Karen Pilosof, Lynn Richardson, Marie Claire Roche, Merle Rosenhek, Joan Sternthal, Marlo Szellos, Jennifer Tanenbaum, Maria Techar, Joanne Thring, Mitty van der Velden, Christine Ward, Carol Weinbaum, Robin Young, Kate Zeidler.

PIA thank the following sponsors and donors for their generous support:

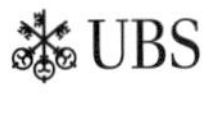

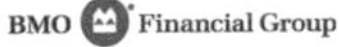

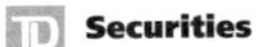 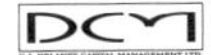

Ray and Berndtson Lovas Stanley

Michelle and Pat Meneley

Amy Kaiser and Ken Rotman

Judy and Larry Tanenbaum and Family

Published in conjunction with the exhibition
'Scott Lyall: THE POWER BALL'
The Power Plant, Toronto
20 September–2 November 2008

The Power Plant
231 Queens Quay West
Toronto, Canada, M5J 2G8

ISBN 978-1-894212-27-4
Printed and bound in Philadelphia.

Publication Editor: Gregory Burke
Assistant Editor: Jennifer Matotek
Texts: Gregory Burke, Caroline Busta, Robert Linsley, Scott Lyall
Design: Claire Christie
Copy Editor: Bryne McLaughlin
Photography Credits:
p. 5-17, Rafael Goldchain (Scott Lyall, THE POWER BALL); p. 18, Helena Reckitt (Scott Lyall,
THE POWER BALL); p. 19-41, Rafael Goldchain (Scott Lyall, THE POWER BALL); p. 42-50,
Steve Payne (Ei Arakawa, THE POWER BALL), p. 51, left to right, top to bottom: Jason Mandella
(Scott Lyall, 'the little contemporaries / Gloria,' courtesy SculptureCenter, Long Island City); Jason
Schmidt (Scott Lyall, 'Plugged and Unplugged,' courtesy Carole Greene and Greene Naftali, New
York); Jason Mandella (Scott Lyall, 'the little contemporaries / Gloria,' courtesy SculptureCenter,
Long Island City); Scott Lyall, 'simple agonie,' courtesy Sutton Lane, London; John Berens (Scott
Lyall, 'a dancer dances,' courtesy Miguel Abreu Gallery, New York); Jason Mandella (Scott Lyall, 'the
little contemporaries / Gloria,' courtesy SculptureCenter, Long Island City); Isaac Applebaum (Scott
Lyall, 'an aaliyah,' courtesy Susan Hobbs Gallery, Toronto); Jason Schmidt (Scott Lyall, 'Washington
Square,' courtesy Carole Greene and Greene Naftali, New York); John Berens (Scott Lyall, 'a dancer
dances,' courtesy Miguel Abreu Gallery, New York); Scott Lyall, 'Belle Epoque'; p. 52-53, Scott Lyall,
'simple agonie,' courtesy Sutton Lane, London; p. 54, Jason Mandella (Scott Lyall, 'the little
contemporaries / Gloria,' courtesy SculptureCenter, Long Island City); p. 55, Miguel Abreu (Scott
Lyall, 'the little contemporaries / Gloria'); p. 56-57, John Berens (Scott Lyall, 'a dancer dances,'
courtesy Miguel Abreu Gallery, New York); p. 58, Isaac Applebaum (Scott Lyall, 'an aaliyah,'
courtesy Susan Hobbs Gallery, Toronto); p. 59, Isaac Applebaum (Scott Lyall, 'The Canon Copiers,'
courtesy Susan Hobbs Gallery, Toronto); p. 60, Jason Schmidt (Scott Lyall, 'Plugged and
Unplugged,' courtesy Carole Greene and Greene Naftali, New York); p. 61, Jason Schmidt (Scott
Lyall, 'Washington Square,' courtesy Carole Greene and Greene Naftali, New York); p. 62-63, Scott
Massey (Rachel Harrison and Scott Lyall, 'When Hangover Becomes Form,' courtesy Contemporary
Art Gallery, Vancouver); p. 64, Scott Lyall, 'Belle Epoque'

Prepress and printing: Brilliant Studio, Exton, PA
Paper: Galerie Art Silk, Mohawk Via
Binding: Bindery Associates, Lancaster, PA
Typeset in Weiss.